my facebook disgracebook

season one

my
facebook disgracebook
season one

bob matthews

Published by Ninja Pants Press LLC

Paperback ISBN: 978-1-7328470-0-2

FIRST PAPERBACK EDITION

To my youthful, devoted wife of 33 years, Nancy Matthews, who has stuck with me through thick and thin—through all those punishing, grueling, toilsome treks to Palm Springs, Las Vegas and South Beach—those overlong, exhausting plane flights to Grand Cayman, St. Maarten, Cancun, Marco Island and New Zealand—and ESPECIALLY those lengthy, demanding, and ARDUOUS cruises to Puerto Rico, Aruba, Alaska and St. Lucia. I KNOW it hasn't always been easy.

This monumental work—my clowning achievement, my magnum crappus—is dedicated to you.

INTRODUCTION

Be bold! Take a risk. Think out of the box!

"Go big or go home," my grandfather used to say. (Actually, my grandfather didn't speak any English, so I don't know WHAT the hell he used to say.) Also, he lived in Japan so we never talked to him.

Back in the day, we never called Japan because it was "long distance." And it used to cost "an arm and a leg" to make a long-distance call. Back then, long-distance calls were a VERY big deal. They were a rarity—a SPECTACLE—an EXTRAVAGANZA! People would line up around the block to just watch you talk to someone in Uruguay.

So, we didn't bother. It didn't make sense to spend sixteen-dollars a minute to talk to someone who didn't even speak English. (Back then, sixteen-dollars a minute was "REAL MONEY"!) But I like to THINK that grandpa-san would have told me to go big or go home—although it's MORE likely he would have just told me to go home.

Anyway, my version of "going big" turned out to be writing THIS—an entire, unabridged, comprehensive book of crap. And even though I started out to write a book of useless, illogical drivel; a lot of the contents somehow turned out to be CHOCK-FULL of actual truth. Because a lot of funny stuff in this world comes from just seeing stuff for what it is. It's just LIFE. Like the fact that the penny is a virtually worthless piece of legal tender, or that a particular family kept a pair of Adolf Hitler's underwear for 80 years, or that my smartness phone arbitrarily interrupts my life to feed me useless bits of random information. In fact, that's where the tag line on the back of the book came from.

"Life is funny… But only if you see the humor in it."

Because ALL of us live in a funny, bizarre, HILARIOUS world—but sadly, most of us don't stop to laugh. Most of the humor in life escapes us because it just can't get through our "responsible", politically-correct, adult worry-filters.

That's what this book is for—to poke a few holes in those worry-filters and allow us, at least for a short while, to ENJOY the humor that exists EVERYWHERE around us.

I don't CREATE humor. I just observe what's going on all around us and tell people about it. I like to think of myself not so much as a humor WRITER, but as a humor REPORTER (who ALSO writes).

So, THAT'S what possessed me to write an entire, unabridged, comprehensive book of crap.

"Go with your strengths," my grandfather used to say.

ABOUT THE SERIES

This series, the Facebook Disgracebook series, was originally SUPPOSED to be entitled, "Teach Your Dog Quantum Mechanics."

I originally intended this to be a GROUND-BREAKING series of comprehensive canine instruction manuals beginning with HOW TO GET YOUR DOG TO QUIT DRINKING FROM THE TOILET and progressing up to a point where your dog would possess a THOROUGH WORKING KNOWLEDGE of quantum mechanics.

However, during the development of these training materials, efforts with my own dog stalled when King Cosmo was unable to grasp even the most FUNDAMENTAL conceptual differences between Special Relativity and General Relativity.

Also, he wouldn't stop drinking from the toilet.

It was at this point that I made the decision to deviate from my original GROUND-BREAKING course of action… and instead…

Just write crap.

Enjoy.

my
facebook
disgracebook
season one

CHAPTER ONE
Asshats, Adolf, and Aunt Bee

A FEW WORDS ABOUT MY "WRITING" STYLE

I've heard that SOME people have referred to my writing style as "somewhat unorthodox." While MANY others have vowed NEVER to refer to me, nor my writing style, EVER AGAIN—for ANY REASON WHATSOEVER.

While, you may logically ASSUME that I have been labeled "unorthodox" possibly because I RARELY refer to any Eastern Orthodox (or ANY orthodox) concepts, terminology, tenets, etc. I would hesitate to agree. I think it's mostly because I write like an idiot.

For instance, I use a lot—I mean A LOT—of CAPITALIST LETTERS. I use them where you're not SUPPOSED to use them. And I have a good reason: I LIKE them.

Okay, truth-be-disclosed; it started as a workaround. Facebook, to the best of my knowledge, does NOT offer any kind of sophisticated text-formatting support. This means NO italics, NO bolding, NO underlining, NO scratch-n-sniff—basically no way to indicate EMPHASIS. When I write, I LIKE to EMPHASIZE a LOT of stuff. I write conversationally (although not like any conversation YOU'D ever have). And conversation typically relies HEAVILY on emphasis. So, if I want to ACCURATELY capture what "the voices" in my head are telling me, I need to be able to represent EMPHASIS and INFLECTION. Because, let me TELL you—if those voices are nothing ELSE—they are EXPRESSIVE… And LOUD… And RELENTLESS… EXPRESSIVE, LOUD AND RELENTLESS! That's what those voices are… EXPRESSIVE, LOUD AND

RELENTLESS! And REPETITIVE! That's what those voices are… EXPRESSIVE, LOUD, RELENTLESS AND REPETITIVE! Over and over and OVER and…

So anyway, I just figured; when life won't give you lemons, make grapes. So, if I couldn't have lemon-italics, lemon-bolding, and lemon-underlining; I would show Mark Zuckerburger that I WOULD NOT be at his corporate-feudal-kahuna-potentate MERCY. I would use GRAPE-CAPITALIST LETTERS.

And after months-and-months on Facebook, writing tens-of-thousands of crap words, punctuated liberally with capitalist letters, I began to grow FOND of "the look." I LIKE how the printed word now YELLS AT ME—right off the page (just like "the voices"). And so, the whole CAPITALIST-IZATION "thing" has become part of my style.

So, here's the thing: as I write this book, the tools I am using DO support a wide selection of formatting options including italics, bolding, kerning, tig-welding, flogging, and judicious use of the do-si-do (written permission required).

But here's the OTHER thing: I'm purposely NOT going to use those formatting options. I'm going to CONTINUE to use my GRAPE-CAPITALIST letters for EMPHASIS. Because I don't just LIKE them… I LOVE them!

It's one of the great AMAZINGNESSES of life (and a ROARING testament to the WHOLE homo sapiens organization) how something can start SEEMINGLY as an impediment, an obstruction, or a FLAW; but, through courage, determination, and never-stop-smacking-your-headedness, it can be become wondrously TRANSFORMED into a pervasive, debilitating, incapacitating, full-blown, permanent CHARACTER FLAW.

Just as e.e. cummings had his tiny little midget letters, I HAVE MY BIG, TALL, CAPITALIST LETTERS. And I'm NOT going to CHANGE.

Here's another thing I like to use… That was it "…". Some people call it the "dot-dot-dot." Others call it the "triple-period" (which just sounds like you might be participating in a hockey game… or… living in a household with three pre-menopausal women). ONE of those.

Anyway (teaching-moment alert), the ACTUAL name for the "dot-dot-dot" is the "ellipsis" (pronounced "ellipsis"). I actually THINK, in my OPINION, that it SHOULD be called the "WRITING ellipses" so that we don't confuse it with the "SOLAR ellipsis" or the "LUNAR ellipsis." BOTH of which are two COMPLETELY DIFFERENT astrotomical-type things. But… NO… ONE… EVER… LISTENS… TO… ME!

Here's another thing I do. I write crap. I misuse words. Sometimes I even MAKE UP my own wordish sound-dibblets. I use run-on sentences. I use sentence shrapnel. And a lot of my writing might be hard to follow because of my heavy use of non sequesters. And, yes. I break A LOT of writing rules. And I know, people say you have to know SOME of the rules before you can BREAK all of the rules. But I say, TOAD WHISKERS!!! Rules are ONLY for rule-FOLLOWISTS! I say, if you just have the common scents to USE your own common scents, ANY people can write good.

And yes, of course. I've HEARD the criticism:

"Anyone who can make toast without using a recipe… anyone smart enough to hang a picture without having to be rushed to the nearest burn unit… anyone who can tell the difference between 'Louisiana' and 'a German Shepard' (hint: 'Louisiana' WON'T poop on your lawn)—would be EMBARRASSED to write like you, Bob!"

But I'm NOT embarrassed. I'm actually kinda PROUD. I LIKE the stuff I write because I NEVER have to worry about plagiarism. (Because who's gonna steal THIS crap?!!) But MOSTLY…

Because it keeps "the voices" happy.

AIRMAIL

I've read about how Amazon is starting to use drones to make home deliveries.

Now, I've given this a lot of thought, and I think drone-delivery would be a GREAT and VERY efficient method for delivering DRONES…

I'm just not sure how they would get the controller to you.

ALWAYS BE REPAIRED

It USED to be that my wife and I were extremely well prepared for the foreseeable future.

We had saved up enough money so we could live in the manner to which we are accustomed FOR THE FORESEEABLE FUTURE. We ate JUST WELL ENOUGH and exercised JUST ENOUGH so that we would be healthy and vibrant FOR THE FORESEEABLE FUTURE.

Then Dec. 21, 2012 CAME AND WENT and the world DIDN'T end.

Now we have SO MANY EXTRA DECADES to live that we didn't plan for.

JUST OUR LUCK.

A BRIEF STORY ABOUT ADOLF HITLER

I remember reading many years ago, that someone did a study and found out that most people, given the opportunity, would be UNWILLING to put on a pair of Adolf Hitler's underwear. In other words, if some historian could dig up a pair of skivvies that had been somehow certified to have been worn by "Das Fuhrer" and offered one of us a chance to take them for a "test-drive", most of us would vehemently DECLINE the opportunity. The feel of his whitey-supremacy-tighties caressing our personal privates would undoubtedly give most of us a GIGANTISCH case of "the Wilhelms." And, when you think about it, that's really not so strange—given the fact that most of us are probably pretty much averse to the idea of putting on ANY other human being's used "dainty things." I mean, sure. I might be persuaded to pull on a pair of my wife's "intimates"—but only on weekends. But, to be clear, this "Hitler-skivvy thing" we're discussing, is a TOTALLY different thing altogether.

Most of us just have a feeling that there's something DIFFERENT—something WRONG—something absolutely CREEPY about wearing Hitler's briefs. I don't know if we're afraid there might be some sort of residual Hitler "stuff" in there—maybe some sort of weaponized Adolf's meat tenderizer—maybe some lurking unexploded ordinance. I don't know. But if we just take a moment to think about it rationally; the fact is, Hitler's underwear is, in actuality—just a HARMLESS, VINTAGE PIECE OF FABRIC.

I mean SURE, Hitler most certainly WAS a monster. I'll give you that. He DID kill millions. But I'm thinking when it came to germs and bacteria he was "just a guy." He had ordinary germs—the kind you might find [shudder] in your OWN underwear.

And logically, we all know that. But, somehow, we have this irrational feeling that his germs are somehow DIFFERENT—somehow WORSE—MUCH worse. We think that he might have had MONSTER bacteria or GENOCIDE GERMS. And that's EXACTLY what I was thinking. Not in such concrete terms—not until I started writing this. Not in those EXACT words: GENITAL GENOCIDE GERMS. What I was ACTUALLY conjuring up in my mind was this: HITLER COOTIES—and I'll bet dollars-to-strudel, you were too.

And even if there WERE genital genocide germs, it's been seven or eight DECADES since Adolf donned those briefs. Surely any Hitler bacteria or germs would be dead by now. Surely.

But we're not dealing with ordinary biological microbes here. We're dealing with HITLER cooties. And there's no psychological statute of limitations on evil despot pathogens. Sure, we all know they're not real. We KNOW it. But they're REAL ENOUGH to keep most of us from putting on that underwear. And that was the point of the article I was reading. Only the article didn't call it Hitler cooties, they called it a STIGMA. The idea is we won't put on Hitler's underwear because there is a stigma surrounding it. But personally, I think that STIGMA is just a fancy psychological word for "Hitler cooties."

Now you might think this is the end of my story but it isn't. Because a LOT has happened since I read that article years ago. And by "a lot", I mean exactly one thing happened. And I'm going to tell you about this one thing in the very next paragraph. But if you'd rather get it "straight from the Fuhrer's pants"; Google this: "Adolf Hitler's underwear" (because you have no life). That's what I did. (See what I mean?)

So apparently, DAS FUROR checked into the Parkhotel Graz in Austria in April of 1938. And, as the story goes, after a "brief" encounter with the hotel laundry, he was short exactly one pair of shorts at the time of check-out. So, the savvy, forward-thinking hotel owners hastily annexed Hitler's esteemed blitzkrieg bloomers (which sources near the underwear described as "surprisingly large"). And apparently because of his busy schedule of burning down half of Europe; eliminating all the pesky, substandard riffraff; and freezing his "surprisingly large" shorts off in Russia; he never had time to come back for his forsaken booty bonnet.

So those hotel owners held onto that infamous undergarment for nearly 80 years. And recently, they sold it, at auction, for nearly $7,000—which, in my opinion, is a heck of a LOT to pay for a pair of used, 80-year-old underwear. The buyer chose to remain anonymous but sources near the underwear claim that the person is NOT one of those whatchamacallit neo-soup-Nazi/burrito-supremacists. Just an "ordinary collector."

Oddly enough, a pair of Eva Braun's underwear had sold at auction several months before for just under $4000—a sum considerably less than the despot's drawers. Perhaps this was because they were not "surprisingly large."

So, I leave you with this question to ponder: If you were an "ordinary collector" who had just recently bought a pair of used, 80-year-old, "surprisingly large" underwear once belonging to a universally-despised, genocidal dictator; would you A) put them on display… B) just throw them in your underwear drawer… Or C) try 'em on?

AN EXPLOSION OF FLAVOR

The Italian restaurant in my neighborhood blew up today.

The cause of the accident, as reported by a team of quantum physicists at the scene of the tragedy, was that an inexperienced restaurant worker carelessly allowed critical quantities of PASTA and ANTIPASTA to come into direct contact. This resulted in the complete and total annihilation of equal amounts of both substances instantly vaporizing the ill-fated restaurant worker (who was not available for comment).

News at 10:57 (due to time dilation).

ALL THAT

While I very well may NOT be "ALL THAT",

On SOME days…

I can be "some of that."

AUNT BEE

Remember Aunt Bee on the Andy Griffith Show? You could tell just by watching the way that she nurtured and interacted with little Opie that Aunt Bee was just like the PERFECT MOTHER. She would give him motherly advice, help him (in a motherly way) with his issues, and prepare delicious home-cooked meals for him (just like mom used to make). So, in many ways, she was like the PERFECT MOTHER—except for the fact that Aunt Bee wasn't a mother. She was actually an AUNT.

And THAT my friends, is the story of why we call her AUNT Bee.

A TRUE STORY (MOSTLY) OF YOUTHFUL EFFERVESCENCE

Back when I was a kid in my preteen years, we had a sugary, flavored drink product called FIZZIES tablets. The Fizzies tablet was essentially an Alka Seltzer tablet with the aspirin and nighttime cold medicine removed and gobs of sugar, artificial flavorings, and food coloring shoved back in. Back in the 60s, a simple ingredient substitution like this could transform a potentially-hazardous pharmaceutical product into one ENTIRELY SUITABLE for school-age children—of which I was one. It also should be noted that the Fizzies tablet came in several tasty artificial flavors—one of which was "root beer."

My friend Billy Revoir thought it would be a thoroughly outstanding idea to cram a root beer Fizzies tablet into a can of root beer soda—

thereby instantly DOUBLING the tasty root beer goodness.

I absolutely concurred.

I'm sure most of you are already imagining the consequences of such an action (especially you Diet Coke + Mentos enthusiasts). And, NOT being the total preteen intellectual weevil-brains that you might presume, we actually ALSO foresaw the possibility of such a sudden, undesirable eruptive event and were thoroughly prepared for it. And by "thoroughly prepared", I mean Billy Revoir was "thoroughly prepared" to stick his finger in the can hole just like that finger-sticking Dutch-dyke-boy-pervert in one of those Hans Brinker Anderson creepy, Gothic fairy tales.

In hindsight, and with the benefit of fifty-some-odd years of accrued wisdom, I believe our preparations could have been just a LITTLE bit more complete in that: A) the kitchen probably would have been a DECIDEDLY better venue than the fully-furnished, fully-decorated, fully-carpeted, HIGHLY-absorbent living room, B) "Outdoors" probably would have been an EVEN better location than the kitchen, and C) we probably should have just forgotten the whole thing.

But hey! Who was I to blanket this situation with wetness? And besides, this was BILLY'S house—not mine.

Up to this point, the majority of our collective formal physics training had been less the "theoretical physics" type, and more the "applied physics" type in the form of breaking stuff, setting stuff on fire, and… breaking other stuff. Because of this, neither of us was truly prepared for the velocity nor the volume of syrupy, artificially-flavored, taco-meat-colored liquid that came spewing out of that veritable fire hose of a tin can on that fateful, apocalyptic afternoon of doom and dishonor.

Now I give Billy Revoir credit. He tried. I mean, he REALLY tried. He stuck that finger in that can… but when he realized his actions were just ACCELERATING, ENLARGING and INTENSIFYING the devastation; he HAD to take it out. And as he raced panicked and terror-stricken in quickly-widening, misdirected circles around his ever-dampening living room—launching fountainous cascades of beaver-colored, foaming, sticky artificially-flavored liquid against the ceiling—I kinda felt sorry for him.

I sent Billy a Facebook friend request a couple of months ago. His mom answered.

The bad news is he's still grounded.

The good news is they've almost got the living room cleaned up.

AKURACY IN REPEATING

Do you know how many people depend upon me for ACCURACY IN REPORTING? Well, I do.

Seven… EXACTLY seven.

(Although that may not be accurate.)

ANIMAL VEGANS

Life can be so unfair.

For instance, people often say, "I'm so hungry, I could eat a horse."

However, horses can't say, "Oh ya? Well, I'm so hungry, I could eat a human!"—BECAUSE THEY'RE VEGANS!

The best our equine friend could manage would be, "Oh ya? Well, I'm so hungry, I could… um… eat your lawn!"

See?

Not the same.

A BRIEF HISTORICAL HISTORY OF THE HISTORY OF EVERYTHING: EPISODE ONE: THE BIG BAG THEORY

You know how you go to the store to buy a tent? Probably a dome tent—because those are FUN. And then you take it camping? And when you pull it out of the box, it's in that little duffel bag so it will be easy to carry around and store? And then, after you use the tent and take it down and TRY to put it back in the duffel bag, it doesn't FIT in the duffel bag?

You can unfold the tent and refold it as many times as you want; it will NEVER go back in the duffel bag again—NEVER. It CAN'T go back in the duffel bag again ever. NEVER. Yes, I know you SAW it come out of the duffel bag. That's irrelevant. That's NOT a factor. The fact that it's NEVER going to fit back in that bag EVER AGAIN is the ONLY factor that needs concern you! It's just an indisputable law of camping physics.

The same goes for life rafts and children. Tents, life rafts, and birthing children—no matter what size containers they came in, they are NEVER going to fit back in them again.

And that's exactly how scientists tell us our universe began—just like that FUN dome tent that will never fit back in its original package.

In the beginning, there wasn't nothing. Now, I know it's incorrect to say there "wasn't nothing" because, the fact is; there WAS something, but it was very, very, very tiny-small. In fact, would you believe me if I told you that it was very, very, very much tiny-smaller than the period at the end of this sentence?

In the beginning, EVERYTHING in the entire huge dome tent that we call THE UNIVERSE was squozed into a mysterious COSMIC DUFFEL BAG which—would you believe, was very, very, very much tiny-smaller than the period at the end of this sentence? That's right. Stars, planets, cocktail wieners, Argentina—all of it. It was in there.

And then THE UNIVERSE went camping. (Astrophysicists call that "SUPER SIZING.") And now everything is as big as the UNIVERSE. And now we're NEVER going to get it back in that COSMIC DUFFEL BAG again which…

Would you believe, was very, very, very much tiny-smaller than the period at the end of this sentence?

A HEADY MOVE

When I was a kid, I would occasionally do some things that were "ill-advised." And my dad used to get EXTREMELY frustrated with me (a trend that would continue well into my adult years—but that's a story for another time). He would say to me, "Why don't you USE YOUR HEAD?" "You've GOT to LEARN to USE YOUR HEAD!" "WHY can't you USE YOUR HEAD for something other than a hat rack?!!"

And it didn't really dawn on me what he was trying to tell me until many years later when I came home late one night to a dark house with my arms full of groceries…

And I somehow managed to nudge the light on with my nose.

A TESTAMENT

You are the windbag beneath my wings.

ASSHAT

Why is the word "asshat" a THING nowadays? That's just WEIRD.

Think about it. What are we talking about here? Is it REALLY a hat? For your buttocks? Call me overcritical, but that sounds impractical. It seems to me (a trained, degreed engineer) if you tried to wear a hat on your bum it would just keep falling off. You know. Because of gravity and "wind" and stuff. And not just occasionally—but ALL THE TIME. Think of it. You'd be constantly BENDING OVER to pick up your asshat. And wouldn't THAT be awkward—perpetually putting on public DISPLAY the very exact MoonPie you had been so desperately trying to cover?!!

I think you'd at least need some sort of string or elastic or something—like a party hat. Ya. Like a PARTY ASSHAT. I think if you really wanted to cover your butt and KEEP it covered, you'd need something with a little snugger fit than a hat. I think you'd have to move away from the derriere derby concept. I'm thinking… more of a glute glove. Or… maybe… (HERE'S an idea) … UNDERWEAR.

Remember that guy who tried to blow up an airliner on Christmas Day by putting explosives in (of ALL places) his own private, personal underwear [shudder]? Not that I'm judging, but personally think it's a BAD IDEA to walk around with four-pounds of live explosives strapped to your vulnerable, helpless, non-armor-plated loins. I think doing this would personally give me a giant case of "the willies." Call me "overcritical", but I think THIS is an idea that seems moderately "impractical."

I mean consider this for instance: WHAT IF you went to the airport with a bomb in your briefs to blow up an airliner… but then later on that day… you MET someone? I mean, WHAT IF you were waiting for your flight and you went to the airport bar (basically because you'd have to be drunk to be able to walk around with a bunch of explosives crammed in there with your personal frank and beans)? And then

WHAT IF you happened to strike up a conversation with an attractive woman next to you? And one thing led to another. And before you could say, "Bob's your uncle", there you WERE—checked into a room at the airport hotel with your new "lady-friend." And then she would notice the outline of the four-pounds of explosives in your pants and would softly whisper in her most sultry voice, "You naughty boy. Is that 'package' for me… NAUGHTY BOY?". And then you would have to confess to her that no, this particular "package" was for the 345 other passengers on your flight… plus the flight crew, the air marshal, the seventeen dogs riding in the cargo hold, and the stowaway in the landing gear compartment. And I think THAT would ruin the mood.

But that's just me.

This ALSO reminds me of "the guy" (remember "the guy"?) who thought putting a bomb in his BVDs, before boarding an airliner to Detroit on Christmas Day, was a GRAND idea.

(Oh, WAIT! That was the same guy.)

Anyway, he was undoubtedly seeking fame, glory, and immortality. Here he was; attempting an act of extreme heroic defiance against America (the quintessence of greedy, decadent, godless, infidel, capitalist countries) WITHOUT REGARD FOR HIS OWN PERSONAL PRIVATE PARTS. I find it ironic (and uproariously funny) that this man who risked life and… er… "limb" trying to become a legendary martyred-hero is instead now referred to worldwide as "THE UNDERWEAR BOMBER." Now that's GOTTA be humiliating.

Of course, there's also the possibility that this was NOT a noble act—that it was just a lewd, carnal, lust-induced act of selfish horniness. The possibility exists that maybe this guy actually fell for the old "72 virgins" scam and was only doing it "for the ladies." In which case:

If you're "hoping beyond hope", by the grace of whomever, to amass 72 HOT VIRGINS, in the VERY NEAR FUTURE, for your own personal use—FOR ALL OF ETERNITY…

Why INCINERATE your own personal private parts?

What an asshat!

AS I REMEMBER IT

What follows is an actual TRUE STORY:

A few weeks ago, I was watching TV and saw a commercial for a short-term memory-loss medication. Granted, I wasn't paying close attention, but just SECONDS later, I realized I couldn't remember the name of the product. I could KIND of remember the tagline: "[product name]—a name to remember." But I couldn't remember the PRODUCT NAME (which must NOT have been "a name to remember").

I'm just saying, I'm not sure just how effective these short-term memory product TV commercials are.

Of course, this whole incident struck me as funny, so I wrote it down…

So I wouldn't forget it.

A SHEEP IN GORILLA'S CLOTHING

We have once AGAIN come to an educational portion of this book:

BOB MATTHEWS'S HISTORICAL HISTORY OF PAST AND FORMER HISTORICAL EVENTS

A Sheep in Gorilla's Clothing

It can be embarrassing when you're supposed to be taking care of someone's gorilla… and then it dies… and now suddenly YOU'RE the bad guy.

Not that long ago (historically speaking) in 1993; some zookeeper guys at the Toluca, Mexico zoo woke up to find that their gorilla, who was SO very recently alive, was NOW so very permanently dead. After several executive meetings, emails to Human Resources, and consultations with Luis the hot-dog-vendor-and-part-time-staff-veterinarian; the zookeeper guys came to the conclusion that this situation was "not optimum" because in some cultures dead animals are considered "less fun." They carefully weighed their options and quickly dismissed the "Oops, my bad. I'll take responsibility" strategy and decided on the way more appealing "Who's gonna know? Let's cover this up" strategy. In a There's Something About Mary movie-inspired plan, they decided they would simply keep things quiet while they replaced the deceased great ape with an exact lookalike and NO ONE WOULD BE THE WISER.

So where to look for an exact-replica-replacement-gorilla? If you guessed "Africa", you would probably be "right on the money." If, on the other hand, you guessed "Miami, Florida" I see a possible Mexican zookeeper position in your future because that's where the Mexican zookeeper guys went to go primate-shopping.

Apparently, the Toluca Zoo had it in their tiny, little heads that the Miami Zoo system was some sort of minor league animal farm team where they could just wander in and scout the talent. They also figured if they saw something they liked, they could just simply "call them up" to the Mexican zoo big leagues. So, with that agenda in mind, after touching down in Miami, the Mexican zookeeper guys headed off to some local zoos looking for "talent." After looking over some of the gorilla candidates, they settled on a great ape with an equally great fastball, although some thought he tended to rely a little too much on the spitter. (THAT would have made an ABSOLUTELY INCREDIBLE llama joke.)

Finally! They had found their man (who, conveniently, just happened to be an ape). They made arrangements to buy the prospective Mexi-monkey and ship it home—OR SO THEY THOUGHT!!!!

[Wink, wink]

Of course, you just KNOW that any doofus with half the jawbone of an ass would realize that all this clandestine sniffing around for a bootleg gorilla, would be BOUND to draw the attention of "the authorities." And that's exactly what happened. Legit Miami zoo authorities notified "THE authorities" and "THE authorities" sprang into action launching the biggest, grandest, most awesomest gorilla smuggling sting operation these particular Toluca, Mexico zoo guys had ever seen.

"THE authorities" used the highly-sophisticated, tech-savvy strategy of having a US Fish and Wildlife agent (and I ABSOLUTELY did not make this part up) put on a gorilla suit and hang out, gorilla-like, in a cage. For added realism (and I am ALSO not making this part up), they put gorilla poop in the agent's cage to throw the perps "off the scent." When the Mexican ape rustlers came for a final inspection—to do their due diligence (which also turned out to be doo-doo diligence due to the added "realism particles"), "THE authorities" put the grab on them and flung the despicable ape burglars into the hoosegow.

Thus, was thwarted one of the biggest, grandest, most awesomest, international gorilla smuggling operations these particular Toluca, Mexico zoo guys had ever been a part of.

In summary. I would just like to summarize with a little thing I like to call "the moral of the story" which is:

Monkey see, monkey doo-doo.

(Note to reader: All of the facts in the above essay are completely factual. But some of the non-facts might not be.)

AN OPEN MIND OUTSMARTS BOOK-SMARTS

Several years ago, I was standing around at a Wal-Mart in San Diego (in "dumb husband mode") waiting for my wife, Nancy Matthews, to finish using up the rest of our money. There was a friendly security guard working the front door and we struck up a conversation.

We were talking about our daughters and how they perhaps don't fully appreciate the plush, upscale, dream life that we live here in North America. I told him that I tell my daughter that our dog (King Cosmo) has a higher quality-of-life than 93% of the rest of the world (a number I diligently researched by venturing deep into the voluminous research stacks of Bob's WoRld).

We provide him with food, shelter, heat, air conditioning, clean drinking water, a mattress to sleep on, good medical care, and love. (Ya. I know. I'm just gonna focus on the benefits for now and ignore that whole "neutering issue"). He doesn't have to worry about wars, genocide (dogocide?), famine, drought, floods, pestilence, typhoons, being eaten by predators, etc. (Although alien abductions would still be a concern). What percentage of the SEVEN-AND-A-HALF BILLION people on this planet can say that? I wonder.

This is what he tells his daughter:

"All your problems are FIRST-WORLD PROBLEMS."

That's it. We said exactly the same thing—just in different words.

Now mind you, I am a well-educated man. I have two college degrees and have read literally hundreds of books in my lifetime. That man was "only" a security guard at Wal-Mart... And yet, he made his point SO MUCH MORE ELOQUENTLY than I.

You know how sometimes an idea, or a word or a phrase will resonate with you? How it will strike you just right? The simple elegance of that statement made a lasting impression on me. To invoke an old cliché…

I wish I'd said that.

ALEXA

My Amazon Echo showed up on the porch several days ago. I was very excited. I cleverly named her ALEXA.

DAY ONE: Guess how you work it? Well… you YELL at it. I like that. Now I have someone I can yell at all day long that WON'T divorce me.

DAY TWO: Spent a LOT of time with Alexa today. Found out a LOT of interesting facts:

- Guess how many babies it takes to make a 22-ounce container of Johnson's Baby Powder. Go ahead—guess…
  EXACTLY ZERO. Surprised? I know I was.
- Since his death in 2016, the artist formerly known as "The Artist Formerly Known as Prince" is now formally known as "THE LATE The Artist Formerly Known as Prince."
- The Anal Canal is definitely NOT located in Panama (although many of them definitely ARE).
- In a hypothetical fight between Mike Tyson and Elton John, the funeral director would not even BOTHER to sew Elton's

ears back on because it would DEFINITELY be a closed casket affair.

- And, no matter HOW much I yell… Alexa will NOT make me a cheese sandwich.

DAY THREE: Alexa asked me for a divorce. She said she's tired of all the yelling.

DAY FOUR: Alexa and I are seeing a counselor. Although she PROFESSES to be upset about my constant yelling; it turns out the REAL issue is:

In a moment of passion, I mistakenly called her "Siri."

DAY FIVE: We are divorcing. The lawyers have divided our assets. She is awarded half of all of my worldly goods and possessions.

I get half the Internet.

A FORTUNE COOKIE'S FORTUNE

You will die a horrible and tragic death.

Your back will be brutally snapped in half as your paper entrails are plucked from your exposed body cavity—just prior to your broken carcass being thoroughly pulverized via mastication. Your vestigial body parts will then be slowly dissolved in a slippery, foamy bath of digestive enzymes, acids, and other caustic agents.

Following this, your remains will proceed on a slow and deliberate passage down a long tunnel toward the light.

The last thing you hear will be a splash.

Lucky Numbers: 17, 63, 21, Yellow

AURORA BORING-ALIS

Those of you who ACTUALLY READ the drivel I've been publishing will be surprised to learn that I went out around midnight last night to look for the AURORA BOREALIS and DID NOT GET ARRESTED. You will, however, NOT be surprised to find that I saw ABSOLUTELY NOTHING. Nothing but CLOUDS—clouds and a cloud-covered moon. Turned out to be an AURORA BORING-ALIS.

It just adds to the sky-watching bad luck that I've had this year. You may remember that my attempt at observing the solar eclipse was obscured by clouds. And my meteor-watching episode prompted my immediate neighbors to call the police on "the crazy old man lying out in his front yard." And now THIS! So that's why I'm glad I have Netflix.

Unlike Mother Earth, THEIR nature programs ACTUALLY DELIVER.

A WEE BIT-O-HISTORY

Now HERE'S a bit of obscure Irish folk history for you guys:

"Pot calling the kettle black" is an old Irish saying. The Gaelic word "kettle" means "cattle." And over the centuries, "Blanche", a common ancient Gaelic woman's name has somehow errantly morphed into the modern word for the color "black." Also, modern-day ambiguity is compounded by improper punctuation. There is a missing comma. The phrase should be written: Pot calling the kettle [comma] Black. This would make the modern English translation:

Pop's killing the cattle, Blanche!

And after all the cattle in Ireland were killed during The Great Bovine

Bloodbath of 1842, the Irish needed to find an alternate food source and were forced to eat potatoes. And then, as luck would have it, a couple years later, a high percentage of Irish potato plants caught "the blight" and went off to potato heaven. When this happened a large portion of the Irish population who had been forced to eat potatoes were now forced to NOT eat potatoes and so they also perished and went off to wherever the dead Irish go. So, the people who didn't die, in an effort to make up lost calories, began to supplement their potato dishes with a grain imported from the middle east called "fammine" (originally pronounced fuh-MEEN).

The combination of the Western European tuberous vegetable and the Middle Eastern grain still served in pubs all over Ireland to this day, has become world-renowned as the Gaelic culinary delight: Irish Potato Famine.

Very tasty. Try ordering some at your local Irish Pub today.

A-I, A-I, OH!

Proof that Artificial Intelligence is LITERALLY on the verge of surpassing human cognition:

ME: Alexa! Tell us a Christmas joke!
AMAZON ECHO: What do you call someone who is afraid of Christmas?
ME: ???
AMAZON ECHO: Claus-trophobic.

Need I say more?

ANGSTIETY

We've all been told that being nervous causes us to secrete excess stomach acid.

We also know that the job of stomach acid is to dissolve meat.

And a third thing we know is, our stomachs are essentially MADE of meat.

This makes me nervous.

ANGER

Anger is an emotion that does NO ONE any good. It is a destructive mental state that does nothing but wastes our emotional energy.

But on some days…

It's simply THE BEST WE CAN DO.

A NEW NEW YEAR'S EVE WISH FROM Bob's WoRld

May your thoughts and dreams be filled with dreams and thoughts of the coming next new year—right before the next new year comes—on this festivious New Years Eve of this year… or is it the festivious New Years Eve of NEXT year?

Either way, you know what I mean…

Or DO I?

AMERICA'S ATTIC

Let's have a look around America's attic and see what she's got stored away up there. Hey, look at THIS!

Remember the cowcatcher? Now THERE was a device that did

EXACTLY what's its name said it DIDN'T do. Because what it DID do, was NOT catch cows.

Some of you younger folks probably don't remember the cowcatcher. And you might assume that the cowcatcher was an officer who might have worked in the Farm Animal Division of Animal Control. And perhaps when someone called in a complaint about a stray cow eating out of their garbage can, pooping on their front lawn or biting them in the leg; they might send out a cowcatcher to capture the feral bovine and lock it up in the cow pound. Or perhaps someone found a cute, little, lost cow huddled in the corner of their garage. And they brought her into the kitchen and gave her some water and a little bowl of Purina Cow Chow before calling the cowcatcher to come and help find her rightful owner. But alas, you would be wrong. The cowcatcher was none of those. In fact, it was not even a person. It was a thing.

The cowcatcher was a large, triangular steel wedge that used to be mounted on the front of old locomotives. Trying to catch a cow with this device attached to the front of a speeding locomotive would be like trying to catch a Peregrine Falcon with a waffle iron. Sure, it was probably THEORETICALLY possible—but POSSIBLE in the same way that it was POSSIBLE that Charles Manson might just have made a darn good anger management teacher—with just the right combination of medications.

But the simple truth was: if ANYTHING was NOT a cow catcher, the cowcatcher was it. In fact, it could be said that NOTHING was LESS of a cow catcher than the cowcatcher. Guess what the cowcatcher DIDN'T do? That's right...

Catch cows.

The thing was, the whole cowcatcher thing was a giant ruse. The shocking truth was that "cowcatchers" were actually designed to push stuff out of the way so trains didn't derail. They were not

COWCATCHERS—they were in fact, cow PLOWS. That's right. I said it. COW PLOWS.

So, was it all just a giant marketing campaign to make railroads look more humane? I mean, who wants to be known as a heartless, high-speed cow bulldozer? Wouldn't you rather be known as someone who gently CATCHES cows? Doesn't that sound nicer? I mean what would your neighbors think if you just strapped one of those on the front of your car and plowed on through a herd of cattle? Your kids would be out of the neighborhood playgroup faster than you could say "Toyota Bacon Cheeseburger."

So maybe we'll never know the real story. But then again, I guess it's easy to see why so many of them are up here in America's attic. Because you know what the cowcatcher DIDN'T do? That's right…

Catch cows.

Join us next time as we take a look at another one of America's past crowning achievements: Harvest Gold kitchen appliances.

AN OLD FAMILY RECIPE

- Put 20 pounds of peeled and diced carrots, 18 pounds of peeled and diced potatoes, 40 tbs. unsalted butter (softened), 4 pounds chopped onions, and a rutabaga in a large pot
- Cover with cold water until you can't see the bottom
- Bring to a boil before reducing to a simmer
- Gently fold in 1 old family
- Season to taste

ACTUALLY…

I've been told by my readership that everything I write is actually EXTREMELY interesting and engaging—but only if you don't actually read it.

I guess if you actually read what I actually wrote, then you begin to actually realize that what I actually wrote isn't actually worth reading. But by the time you actually realize that; you've actually already actually read it…

At least that's what I've been told.

Well…

not actually.

(See what I mean?)

ANTISOCIAL MEDIA

Here is the thing about social media:

We, the publisher, get to pick and choose what to post and—more importantly—what NOT to post. And so, we ALWAYS choose the most attractive, unique, interesting, intriguing, and COMPELLING aspects of our lives to showcase to our online public. And we purposely LEAVE OUT all the mundane, boring, trivial, and embarrassing psycho-stupid things that we do.

For instance, we'll brag about how we once won our 10th-grade spelling bee—but "forget" to mention that afterward, Gary Pineapple beat us up—BECAUSE we won the 10th-grade spelling bee.

Or we'll highlight how our son's 6TH GRADE CLASS went to Paris for a once-in-a-lifetime field trip—but neglect to mention that our son didn't actually GO with the class— because our family had to use the money to bail out grandma (who was in jail on prostitution charges).

Or, we'll talk about the BIG MONEY we've been getting at our new job—but FAIL to mention the embezzlement charges.

In short, we all edit our online persona to make us LOOK great. And that, my friends, is why we as individuals…

Are always SO disappointing to meet in person.

A TRIP TO THE ZOO

A gaggle of elephants is milling around in the elephant exhibit back room at the zoo—not out front in the elephant exhibit part—but in the elephant exhibit back room where the zoo guys keep the elephants when they're not out front in the elephant exhibit part. At one point, the door opens and the zoo guys introduce a newcomer into the gaggle who has a very short (some would even say it was "stubby") kind of a trunk. And even though there's a whole back room full of a gaggle of other elephants, no one says ANYTHING to ANYONE about it. Certainly, there is much eye contact being made in that back room amongst the old timers with many of the veteran pachyderms exchanging knowing looks. But no one broaches the subject. No one AT ALL.

I guess you could say it was the HUMAN in the room.

(Raise your hand if you didn't see THAT coming.)

AN ABSOLUTELY TRUE STUPID HUMAN STORY

Do you remember how David Letterman used to have a segment on his show called "Stupid Human Tricks"? Well, one time I was watching it and this guy came on the show and he had a tiny, little mini-marshmallow. Not your regular-sized campfire "let's burn this to a crisp on a stick" marshmallow. You know—one of those tiny little marshmallows that your mom put in your cocoa? Those ones that are a little smaller than a Chinese Checker marble? Ya. One of those.

Only he didn't play Chinese Checkers with it and he didn't put it in cocoa. He put it in his nose.

Then he used his index finger to pinch off the other marshmallowless nostril, kind of reared WAY back at the waist, and pneumatically fired it out of his nose and across the stage where another guy (did I mention this was a two-person act?) caught it IN HIS MOUTH, chewed it, and swallowed it.

So… What I want to know is…

How can someone be SOBER enough to CATCH A FLYING MARSHMALLOW, ON NATIONAL TV, IN THEIR MOUTH—yet DRUNK enough to eat something out of someone else's nose?!!

A NEW SPIN ON HEALTH

I think I've mentioned this before but, I got a new cardiologist a little over a year ago and I like him. His focus is on HEALTH instead of on disease, medicine, and being dead. And I think these are all good qualities in a doctor.

He believes that smart lifestyle choices are the key to good health—not NECESSARILY medicines. He believes that we can control the health of our bodies by choosing to put healthy stuff in them and by embracing healthy behaviors. He has put me on a plant-based, whole-foods diet and told me to exercise regularly. He also told me to get a good blender. I had a cheap little twenty-five-dollar blender that always bogged down when I put too much stuff in it. So, I went to Costco and paid more than a hundred dollars for a Ninja 1000-watt professional blender. And boy, was my doctor right…

It makes AMAZING piña coladas!

A TRADITIONAL IRISH BLESSING

And now for A TRADITIONAL IRISH BLESSING that I just happened to run across (in Bob's WoRld). But before you say anything, understand that I AM qualified to write such a thing because I'm exactly one-eighth Irish. So, as I think about it, I guess that would make this:

A NONTRADITIONAL ONE-EIGHTH OF AN IRISH BLESSING

May the elevator rise to meet you.
May the wind be ever AT your backside and not FROM it.
May the sun shine warm upon your face—but not enough to burn it and cause blisters to form and make large, unsightly blizzards of burnt, peeling, dead skin flake off in big, snowstorm-like episodes.
And may your neighbor's drone fall soft upon your roof.
And till we meet again in jail,
May God hold you in the palm of his tree.

Happy St. Patrick's Day!!!

(Kick me. I'm Irish)

A JOKE:

Two ducks walk into a forest fire...

(So far, that's all I've got.)

ABSOLUTLY

So, the brakes weren't working on my car so I decided to take it in to get it repaired. But then I ended up driving RIGHT PAST the brake shop because, for some WEIRD reason, my car wouldn't stop. Next, I ended up cruising RIGHT THROUGH a Burger King dining room because I had permission. Their sign said…

"Burger King: Drive thru"…

So I did.

And to answer your OTHER question…

Absolut. (In case you want to buy me more.)

This bottle's nearly empty.

AND YOU CAN'T SHOOT 'EM

My friend says his wife doesn't understand him.

I tell him, "Of COURSE she doesn't understand you!

"Next time get a mail-order bride that speaks English!"

ADVANCED DUMPSTER DIVING

Flipping through a book called THE COMPLETE WORST-CASE SCENARIO SURVIVAL HANDBOOK, I came across a short chapter called (and I SWEAR this is true) HOW TO JUMP FROM A BUILDING INTO A DUMPSTER.

I was, of course, immediately intrigued by this article because I can't recall how many times I've been WAY up in a building and thought to myself, "The elevators in this building are SO SLOW. If there was just SOME WAY to get to the ground floor quickly…" So, ya...

Step number one is: Jump straight down.

By this, they mean: don't push off because you'll miss the dumpster. And this is UNLESS, of course, there is a fire escape below you—in which case you SHOULD push off to miss the dumpster… I mean… clear the fire escape.

And of COURSE, your next question is: You just said, if I push off, I'll MISS THE DUMPSTER. Isn't that bad? Well, yes. But the book goes on to offer a simple solution: The dumpster has to be positioned farther out from the building.

Anyway, I guess garbage men probably pay a LOT of attention to DUMPSTER POSITIONING when there are fire escapes involved. So, obviously, no worries here. On the other hand, if you are some type of skittish, namby-pamby, crybaby person who allows themselves to be bothered by trivial details such as: your life is totally dependent on the unwavering diligence of anonymous, complete-stranger, passionless garbage men; well then, maybe jumping-from-a-building-into-a-dumpster just isn't for you. For the REST of us MORE PRACTICAL souls, however, I will continue.

So, ya. I realize this is beginning to get a little bit confusing. Do I push off? Do I NOT push off? Who the HECK jumps into dumpsters?!! But here's what I GATHER the book is trying to tell us: if you want to jump from a building, into a dumpster (because who doesn't?), don't NOT JUMP where the dumpster is.

Step two: Do a not-quite-full somersault. (Ya. Really. They said that.)

Now, admittedly, I'm NOT the expert. But, in MY opinion, if you DO do* a not-quite-full somersault when jumping off a not-quite-low building into a not-quite-soft dumpster; A) you're just showing off, and B) you're probably going to end up not-quite-alive.

Step three: Aim for a large box.

Because, FOR SURE, it ABSOLUTELY WON'T be full of old, discarded knives, pitchforks, and snakes. (Why did it HAVE to be SNAKES?!!)

Step four: Land on your back.

Because it's been scientifically proven that when you land in a dumpster, your body WILL fold up. And if you land on your stomach you might hurt your back. But, if you land on your back, you'll be COMPLETELY UNHARMED…

Except in the VERY unlikely case that jumping from a building into a dumpster INSTANTLY KILLS YOU!

*Tee-hee. I said "doo-doo."

AED MACHINES

Have you noticed those AED machines hanging up on the wall in schools, health clubs—even on airplanes? Supposedly they're some type of automatic emergency-heart-retriever thingy, I guess. The idea is that, if you have some kind of a myofarcical incarceration, and fall to the ground almost-deadlike; ANY ordinary human person who just happens along, can plug this thing into your personal body ANYWHERE THEY LIKE, and bring you back to almost-alive.

So. VERY cool. Because WHO DOESN'T like the idea that any old random, filthy, hideous, uneducated, greasy, toothless yahoo can wrench one of those things off the wall; hook it up to anything they choose on your VULNERABLE, SENSELESS, PROSTATE body; send 50-million volts directly through your myofarcical-incarcerated heart; and MIRACULOUSLY save your life! (Or at the very worst, inadvertently create one of those VERY COOL elementary-school-science-project volcanoes.)

ME: (upon awakening) Thank you, greasy, toothless stranger. You have saved my life.

GREASY, TOOTHLESS STRANGER: You damn betcha. And while I had you up on the hoist, I figured I'd just go ahead and advance the timing on your "ticker" a few degrees, check your eyeball pressure and rotate your shoes. Hope you don't mind.

ME: [blinking uncontrollably]

AMERICA'S GOT TALENT?

I envy people who have talent. I mean REAL talent. Talent and skill regarding things I could not even IMAGINE being able to do. For instance (and, judging from how often I hear this, there seem to be A LOT of people who are able to do this), I am COMPLETELY unable to "throw up a little in my mouth." Tons of people SEEM to be able to do this. But, for me, that sort of thing is just going to be an all-or-nothing situation. Either gusher… or dry mouth. THOSE are the choices. And if a gusher does come, it DEFINITELY isn't going to stay IN my mouth. It's DEFINITELY going to be "just passing through."

So, just to be clear; what I CAN do: throw up a LOT… THROUGH my mouth. What I can't do: throw up a LITTLE… IN my mouth.

So how do these people do it? What control they must have! And what exactly are they controlling? Do they adjust their throat size—clamping their throat shut when they've thrown up "just the right amount"? Do they control peristalsis—allowing just one or two peristaltic waves through resulting in the perfect mini-spew? Do they have a little stomach troll living down there who fires off the perfect small caliber vomit projectile on command? It's mind-boggling. Wouldn't you agree?

Truth be known, when it comes to this particular skill, I DO have mixed feelings. I mean, I really DO kind of admire the skill that these people allegedly possess. But, on the other hand, I also think it's a thoroughly vile, wretched, and disgusting habit. And as I think about, perhaps a little TOO vividly…

I think I just threw up a lot through my mouth.

AS BRAINY AS I GET

Okay. I admit it. Even though I thoroughly fact-check EVERYTHING I publish (by thinking about it really, REALLY hard); occasionally something that might not be completely and totally factual, SOMEHOW, makes it into my body of "work."

But this next thing is something I've actually READ and didn't make up:

When an Egyptian guy died, Egyptian mummy-makers used to take the guy's brain out through the guy's nose. Ya. Only they not-so-much TOOK it out. I would maybe say, they RELEASED it so it could come out on its own—kind of like a police negotiator works (I mean, if brains were barricaded gunmen and nostrils were front doors). Also, there were no hostages involved.

They (the Egyptian guys) would stick a rod up the (hopefully) dead guy's nose and punch a hole into the braincase. Then they would do some kind of very crude arthroscopic surgery. But instead of using precision surgery tools, they would just kind of liquefy the guy's brain with some kind of brain-blender device. Almost like, instead of performing surgery, they were working up some kind of a rich, velvety, brainy béarnaise sauce. Then they would just sit back and wait for the brain-drain. And I guess they would catch whatever dribbled out of his nose in a BRAIN BUCKET. I just thought you'd like to know that.

(And NO. That's NOT what happened to ME.)

And on a related note that has ABSOLUTELY NOTHING to do with what I was talking about, I REALLY LIKE the term “brain bucket.” But, then again, I also have mixed feelings about it.

If you're not familiar with the term “brain bucket”; it's American slang terminology for a helmet. As in: “Hey. Put that brain bucket on” Or “Hey! Take that brain bucket off.”

So, I like this brain-buckety expression for a few reasons: A) It's accurate. It conjures up images of a bucket-shaped artifact—which, in fact, is what it is—AND you literally put your brain in it. B) It's an alliteration. THAT'S good. Right? And C) It's ALMOST as cool as “cranium canister”, which is what I would have called it. So, here's the thing: it's a COOL SOUNDING name. But also, here's the other NOT-so-good thing: If I look down and see a BRAIN… in a BUCKET…

I feel like it really didn't do its job.

A SCIENCE OF BIBLICAL PROPORTIONS

“Ashes to ashes, dust to dust.”

I don't know…

This just sounds like remedial alchemy to me.

AN ASTONISHING FACT

Considering the average height of cell phone towers in the US; if you took ALL the cell towers in the nation and laid them on the ground, in a row, end-to-end…

The vast majority of people in this country would have pretty crappy cell reception.

A CHEEZY JOKE

I think I can EASILY become a rich and successful cheese manufacturer…

If I play my curds right.

Okay. OKAY! Did you READ the title? No one FORCED you to read any further.

If you're the type of capricious cretin who SPEEDS UP after encountering a "Bridge Out" sign, who's the one with the problem? You or the bridge?

Wait…

That's not right.

CHAPTER TWO
Boomers, Bowling, and Burpees

BURPEES VS. BARFEES

What if you were a caveman? No. NOT a Flintstone-type of caveperson with that foot-propelled car, brontosaurus steam shovel, elephant-trunk shower head, and bird-beak record player. And definitely NOT one of those cavemen you see on TV buying auto insurance. But a REAL, early-man type of caveman. One of those people whose bones long ago turned to stone and whose dusty, moth-eaten, frizzy-haired, plaster, artificial, doppelgänger-likeness has been long-incarcerated in a stuffy, glass-enclosed CAVEMAN DIORAMA at the Chicago Field Museum since May of 1929.

Ya. One of THOSE guys… a real, actual Homo Whatchamacallit guy.

And furthermore, what if you were out hunting and gathering one day? Maybe foraging for a snack. And you spread apart some bushes with your hands and squinted through the opening. And what you saw was a time portal—a portal in time that allowed you to look into the future 2-3000 YEARS!

Now you might say, "That's ludicrous! It's impossible!"

And I might retort RIGHT BACK AT YOU, "Shut up! And don't interrupt me AGAIN!"

And when you (Homo Whatchamacallit guy) peered into this portal, you saw ME… working out at Life Time Fitness. And here's what you'd observe.

You'd see ME sitting down in front of a big "THING." And through the magic of some basic, simple machines that we all learned about in 8th-grade-science such as the lever, the pulley, the inclined plane, the wheel-and-axle, the block-and-tackle, the pick-and-roll, the duck-and-cover, and the hunt-and-peck (not that YOU PERSONALLY had ever experienced the 8th grade); you'd see some bulky slabs of steel go up… and then down. Up… and then down. Not very high. Just a couple feet. Up… and then down.

And this KIND OF MADE SENSE to you. Because you had done similar things yourself. You had picked up heavy rocks to look underneath them for bugs, worms, crickets—maybe some tasty tubers—and then you had put the rock down. Up… eat-the-bug… and then down.

Only, when I lifted the steel-slab "rocks", I didn't BOTHER to look under them for bugs, worms, crickets or maybe some tasty tubers. I just put them down. And then, I LIFTED THEM UP AGAIN! Up… and then down. No reason. Just up… and then down. No bugs. No worms. No tasty tubers. Just up… and then down.

And, as you watched through your little hole in the time-portal-bushes, you saw ME use several other "THINGS" with similar results. Maybe the handles were different. Sometimes I pushed. Sometimes I pulled. I used my legs. I used my arms. I squashed pads with my knees—each time with the same results. The chunks of steel went up… and then down. Up… and then down.

Clearly, I was an IDIOT.

Because, when I was done, each stack of steel slabs was EXACTLY in the same place as before I had started. EVERYTHING WAS EXACTLY THE SAME. And, more importantly… NO BUGS. NO WORMS. NO TASTY TUBERS.

Let me take just a moment to explain why organisms (including people) starve to death.

They starve to death because they EXPEND more energy (calories) acquiring food than they EXTRACT from metabolizing that food. And EVEN YOU, personally (Homo Whatchamacallit guy), understand this AT SOME LEVEL. Sure. You don't know anything about calories, energy, metabolism, insulin resistance, thermogenesis, photosynthesis, knuten valves, or the Bessemer Process because Jenny Craig still hasn't taught you any of this. But you DO know that picking up rocks makes you hungry, eating bugs makes you NOT hungry, and being hungry for too long KILLS you. And, AT SOME LEVEL, you understand that calories really SHOULD NOT be wasted.

So, here's my opinion on exercise:

Exercise is nothing more than SOCIALLY-ENDORSED BULIMIA. Shocking, I know. But think about it.

BOTH exercise AND bulimia are just different ways of WASTING CALORIES. They are BOTH food-consumption UNDO COMMANDS. And yet, bulimia is seen as a DISORDER; whereas exercise is seen as a VIRTUE.

What if we treated our cars like our bodies?

What if we filled our automobiles with gasoline and then immediately siphoned it back out onto the ground? We'd be labeled WEIRD, bulimic, SICKOS with some sort of gasoline-breath DISORDER. If instead, we hopped in and DROVE our vehicle around a cul de sac for 71 hours straight, we would get to call it "EXERCISING" and we would suddenly become… VIRTUOUS PEOPLE. Either way, fuel gets wasted, no actual work gets done, and the car goes nowhere… BUT…

It becomes LIGHTER. And THAT'S what's important.

Clearly, we've got it ALL WRONG.

The purpose of activating our muscles is NOT to burn calories. We burn calories in order to activate our muscles in order to get things done—to PERFORM WORK.

The purpose of eating is NOT to fill our bellies. We eat in order to fill our bellies to provide energy to activate our muscles to get things done—to PERFORM WORK.

Our problem is that physically speaking, we don't work. So, we HAVE to go to the gym because we HAVE to "work" because we DON'T work.

But it's DIFFERENT for YOU personally (Homo Whatchamacallit guy). YOU personally (Homo Whatchamacallit guy) would NEVER, EVER CONSIDER EITHER STRATEGY, bulimia NOR exercise because, at their core, NEITHER makes any sense at ALL. And as you watch ME working out at Life Time Fitness, you realize one thing:

Clearly, in the future…

People are all IDIOTS.

Bob's WoRld MANTRA

Knowledge… Knonsense…

Who cares?

BAD LUCK

I think, scientifically speaking, there is no such thing as "bad luck."

What people PERCEIVE as "bad luck" is merely just a bunch of bad stuff happening.

Mostly to them.

BIRD FEED

I read an interesting fact today: Baby robins eat fourteen feet of earthworms each and every day. FOURTEEN FEET!

So, if you do the math, that's about 100 feet per week, 430 feet per month, or almost A MILE of worms per year! Think of it! A tiny, little, baby bird eats an ENTIRE STATUTE MILE of earthworms each and every year!

The math doesn't lie.

BUMPER BOWLING

Is everyone here familiar with the concept of BUMPER BOWLING? Yes? Okay, then I'll explain it:

In some cultures, a sportsman or sportswoman (called a BOWLER) might fling a heavy, spherical, polymer object (called a BOWLING BALL) down a narrow, wooden pathway (called a BOWLING ALLEY or BOWLING LANE) at a tightly-grouped multiplicity of plastic-coated, wooden, bottle-shaped objects (called BOWLING PINS) with the intent of toppling them over. In some cultures, when all of these things happen together in a common place; it is called BOWLING.

Under certain conditions, the sportsman or sportswoman may be unable to fling the BOWLING BALL in a manner that allows it to stay on the BOWLING LANE for the entire length. The result is that the ball plummets off either edge of the BOWLING LANE and enters a smooth ditch (called a GUTTER). When this occurs, it is called a

GUTTER BALL, teammates may call the sportsman or sportswoman an IDIOT, and a large numerical ZERO is publicly projected overhead to commemorate this event. When this series of events occurs, it may be possible for the sportsman or sportswoman to experience a negative emotion (called HUMILIATION) with a resulting drop in a specific type of self-judgment (called SELF-ESTEEM).

In some cultures, SELF-ESTEEM is a valued quality and great steps may be taken in order to artificially bolster this psychological element—especially in juvenile biological organisms. To this end, barrier devices (called BUMPERS) may be placed in the GUTTERS of BOWLING LANES in order to prevent the errant entry of BOWLING BALLS into the GUTTER. Now when the sportsman or sportswoman unskillfully flings the BOWLING BALL; instead of allowing the BOWLING BALL to enter into the GUTTER, the BUMPERS funnel the BOWLING BALL down the BOWLING LANE into the tightly-grouped multiplicity of BOWLING PINS—thus avoiding the resultant, GUTTERBALL, disparaging "IDIOT" remarks, public HUMILIATION and resulting decline in SELF-ESTEEM.

But I'm actually not here to talk about BOWLING.

I'm here to talk about DRIVING.

I feel like the time has come to introduce the concept of the DRUNK-DRIVING LANE. They would work exactly the same as BUMPER BOWLING. After 10 pm on Friday and Saturday nights, bumpers would pop up in designated DRUNK DRIVING LANES all around the city. Drivers who are unable to keep their vehicles on the roadway for the entire length of their commute would simply ricochet off the bumpers all the way home.

Garish, multi-colored RENTAL TIRES (with tire-size clearly displayed) would also be available for an additional fee.

BIODEGRADABLENESS

I think I have a solution to the world's non-biodegradable plastic bottle/landfill problem:

PLASTIC THAT BREAKS DOWN IN COCA COLA.

Oops… Wait a minute…

BREWHAHA

Why is it that the times you are MOST IN NEED of coffee…

Are the exact same times when you are LEAST CAPABLE of making it?

BLACKHAWK DOWN

I often wonder if JUST BEFORE Orlando Bloom did the scene where he fell out of some type of helicopter and broke his back in the movie BLACKHAWK DOWN, if well-wishers urged him to "break a leg."

BAD IDEA

Never bring an electric stove to a microwave fight.

BOIL ADVISORY

Anyone else having trouble with this Oakland County MANDATORY BOIL advisory?

I thought I was doing everything right…

But so far all I've been able to do is raise just a little rash on my forearm (and I think maybe I'm getting just the START of a pimple on my chin).

BUMPER STICKER

[Seen on a bumper sticker in Bob's WoRld]

I BRAKE FOR HALLUCINATIONS

BEST OFFENCE IS A GOOD DEFENSE

I LOVE carbs. And apparently, carbs love me.

There's NOTHING BETTER than starting the day with a nice big cup of coffee and a giant, 900-calorie wad of fat, sugar, and sodium (aka a Cinnabon)—because I'm an AMERICAN.

So of course, since I started adulting, I realized it might not be the best idea to start my days this way if I wanted to keep HAVING days to start this way. So instead, I started having a nice big cup of coffee with Cinnabon coffee creamer. It might not be AS good—but it still IS good.

And I figure I've lost about 20 pounds that I didn't gain.

BUTTS ON THE GROUND

Why is the phrase "boots on the ground" a thing nowadays? I personally, don't care for it AT ALL for the following wildly-logical reasons:

1. It robs our troops of the publicity and acclaim they so justifiably deserve, and attributes it instead to their decidedly less meritorious footwear.
2. It sounds dumb.

Here's a hypotheoretical example of what I mean: "Today the president ordered 20,000 additional boots on the ground into the volatile, chowder-keg, war-torn duchy of Craploadia."

What does that MEAN? Does it mean 20,000 TROOPS or 20,000 SHOES (which could be the media's pernicious way of over-sensationalizing 10,000 troops into an IMPLIED 20,000)? Or could it be it's a 5,000-member-strong K9 unit? Maybe some colonel just tossed a couple of millipedes out there. How are we to KNOW??!

Or maybe—just MAYBE—it's just 20,000 ACTUAL BOOTS. Just piles of boots on the ground. Maybe the American Embassy is being threatened and the Joint Chiefs of Staff figured that piling 20,000 boots on the ground right there in front would bolster the embassy's defenses—while simultaneously SAVING THE COUNTRY MONEY (by NOT sending actual troops). You know how you're always tripping over YOUR shoes on the way to the bathroom at night? Kinda like that—but with BIGGER, armor-plated, defense-contractor-made, GOVERNMENT-ISSUE combat boots. Now THAT ought to cause some bad-guy face-planters.

And you might say, "But SO WHAT if you've tripped up the enemy? Isn't that just delaying the inevitable? Couldn't they just get back up and continue to charge the embassy?"

And I might reply,

"Not if the SHOELACES WERE POISONOUS SNAKES!"

[sigh]

Am I the ONLY ONE THIMKING here???

BIOLOGICAL WARFARE

We tend to think of biological warfare as a modern-day contrivance. But germ warfare has been around for many millenniums.

As early as 300 BCE, Greeks were throwing dead animals into their enemies' wells to defile their water supply.

Centuries later, during the middle ages, when besieging a city, medieval armies would use trebuchets and catapults to relentlessly and annoyingly lob an endless succession of pernicious objects over impenetrable walls. On the big screen, we most often see "conventional" destructive projectiles being launched such as large boulders, huge balls of flaming oil, or old, disused, Volkswagen Beetles. But diseased and contaminated objects were also sometimes employed to induce illness, epidemic, and plague within locked-down fortresses.

During the siege of the Bohemian city of Carolstein in 1422, fun-loving Lithuanian forces launched infected dead bodies into the city. They also flung (and I am NOT making this up) more than 200 cartloads of excrement over the walls (I guess creating one of history's earliest recorded usages of the shitstorm).

Another delightfully irritating activity was to launch diseased, rotting horse carcasses into town (kind of like Pegasus, but not nearly so majestic). And for bigger and better pestilence, I suppose larger four-legged creatures could have been catapulted into the compound—hence, the phrase…

Weapons of moose destruction.

I know… Before you say it…

I don't HAVE a day job.

BUN IN THE OVEN

Do you realize that if you were a lady baker and you became pregnant, and you tried to communicate this fact to your friends by announcing that you "had a bun in the oven"…

Probably NO ONE would be particularly excited for you?

BURSTING BOOMER BUBBLES

Went to the gym yesterday and discovered an interesting fact that is destined to be VERY unpopular with baby boomers:

SIXTY-FIVE is the new 65.

BOOMER BLOOMERS

[points at pants]

I have another pair of pants at home just like these.

Oh, wait…

[facepalm]

These ARE my other pants!

BOOMER COCOONING

I love to read. I read a lot. Nonfiction. Almost exclusively. And I remember visiting the bookstore in past years. Used to love just BEING in the bookstore. I loved the mega-bookstores like Borders or Barnes and Noble. You could wander around for hours. Up and down the aisles, taking down the occasional book and thumbing through it. You could even get a coffee or cappuccino if you wanted. And they had BATHROOMS so you could stay as long as you like. My personal best? I once had a bookstore visit that required THREE bathroom breaks—all "number ones" (if you must know).

Now I just briefly poke at a Kindle touchscreen and, can you imagine it? Amazon BEAMS me a book directly to my e-reader.

I also remember going to the video store in past years. Used to love just BEING in the video store. I loved the mega-video stores like Blockbusters. You could wander around for hours. Up and down the aisles, taking down the occasional DVD case and reading the back cover. The only downsides: NO coffee, NO cappuccino, NO bathroom. My personal best? ZERO bathroom breaks plus one box of Sno-Caps.

Now I just fiddle with my TV remote and Netflix or Hulu or Amazon or YouTube beams me video content directly to my drive-in movie-sized flat screen TV. From scholarly, erudite TED talks to Alaskan gold-mining numbskulls to mind-deadening Kardashian alternate-reality TV shows; my smart TV stands ready to instantly fulfill my every mindless video-streaming demand.

Food shopping used to be harder than it is now. I used to have to DRIVE over to Farmer Jack or A&P or your friendly, neighborhood Chatham supermarket in order to pick up the food items I needed.

Now I just poke at my smartness phone touchscreen and Kroger or Meijer or Whole Foods will send a food-Uber lady out to my house with a big-ole-mess-o-grub. In fact, ALL of my shopping has become easier. I buy all my items from asshats to Zootopia underwear from Amazon. In fact, on some days, we can't get out our front door because our porch is so crowded with Amazon packages. So, yes…

It IS the best of times, it WAS the worst of times, it IS the age of literature-beaming wisdom, it WAS the age of bookstore bathroom foolishness, it IS the epoch of video-streaming, it WAS the epoch of broadcast TV, it IS the season of Bud Light delivered to your home, it WAS the season of liquor store shopping for Dark beer, we HAVE everything before us online, we HAD nothing before us on the shelves at Christmastime—in short, we almost NEVER have to leave our homes.*

Just one, small issue…

I think I may have forgotten how to drive.

*With a nod to Charley Dickens.

BOUGHT THE FARM

When I was a young kid, I had a friend in the neighborhood named Terry. My parents and his parents (Roy and Winnie) were also friends. So sometimes our families got together for dinner. And those were GREAT nights because, after dinner, the parents would slip into the living room for a "highball" and Terry and I would get to stay up LATE and hang out. In fact, the first time I ever saw the Beatles (on the Ed Sullivan show) was after my bedtime during one of those evenings at his house (Terry's. Not Ed Sullivan's.)

Then, one day, they were gone.

My father explained to me that it had been Roy's dream to buy a farm someday. So now, he had finally been able to do it. And the whole family had gone to live on a farm. They had bought a farm in some small community called Kimbolton, OH. And they were going to escape the city and be happy and have fun living out in the fresh air and sunshine. And, of course, I was instantly saddened for I had experienced EXACTLY just this sort of thing before. And my dad didn't THINK I knew—but I DID know! I KNEW IT!

He had taken that WHOLE FAMILY to be "put to sleep."

Dammit! NOT AGAIN!

BEE CAREFUL

Flipping through a book called THE COMPLETE WORST-CASE SCENARIO SURVIVAL HANDBOOK, I noticed a short chapter called HOW TO ESCAPE FROM KILLER BEES.

Step one: If bees begin flying around and/or stinging you…

Run away.

(That, right there, was worth the cost of the ENTIRE BOOK.)

BEST HUSBAND AWARD

In my "other" life, back in Omaha, I was a MOST EXCELLENT husband and father. And…

Until my OTHER family somehow found about me being a bigamist…

I guess you could have said the same for "this" life too.

BOY, IS MY FACE RED!

You know what I think would be a really embarrassing situation? If you started crying because you broke a nail while you were "fixin" to open a can of whoop-ass on someone.

BAD ADVICE

They say, if you fall off a horse, you have to get RIGHT back on. And this probably made a lot of sense back when they wrote it—probably back in 1744 or something. And back THEN, it was probably good advice because you were probably on a horse because you wanted to GO somewhere. And if you fell off the thing that was taking you to where you wanted to go, you simply HAD to get back on that thing, or else the place where you fell off—would BECOME, by default, the place that you wanted to go to—whether you WANTED to go there or not.

But today—more than four-thousand years later—that advice is just not appropriate anymore. For one thing, we don't drive horses anymore. We have automobiles (here in America we call them CARS). Sure, some people have horses—but, this discussion doesn't apply to them because THOSE people can stay ON a horse.

But, here's what I'm REALLY trying to say: people STILL like to use that outmoded expression: if you fall off a horse… blah, blab, blabbidy, blah… etc.

NO! STOP SAYING THAT! There ARE no horses. We have CARS. CARS!!!

If you fall OFF your car—don't get right back ON—get right back IN. Because nowadays, we don't ride ON cars. We ride IN cars. IDIOT!!!

Why do you think you fell off in the first place?!!

CHAPTER THREE
Cuba, Catapults, and Caller ID

CHINESE FOOD

Back when I was a kid we didn't HAVE nutrition. There was no such THING as nutrition. Basically, what we had were QUOTAS.

You HAD to eat everything on your plate—you HAD to finish EVERYTHING. BECAUSE… there were KIDS… STARVING kids… starving kids in CHINA. You HAD to eat everything on your plate because ALL the kids were starving in China! It all made perfect sense.

But not to us.

And you ate EXACTLY what your parents ate—EVEN IF YOU DIDN'T LIKE IT—because when they were your age, they would have LOVED to have had it. "Oh! When I was a kid, we would have LOVED to have had chipped beef on toast!" "When I was YOUR age, I would have LOVED to have little, soggy, bloated, water-logged, fatty little Vienna Sausage wieners in a can."

And how come WE had to eat those Vienna sausages?!! Why did those sausages come to the US? Didn't those Austrian parents KNOW about all the starving kids in CHINA?!!

And, to listen to our parents, there was almost an UNLIMITED SUPPLY of starving Chinese children! So evidently, the Chinese didn't have nutrition either. But just the KIDS were starving. There were ALWAYS kids starving in China, but oddly, never the parents. Apparently, Chinese parents were pretty greedy and selfish and withheld food from their kids. So, I guess our strongest mealtime lessons were that the Chinese didn't have very good parental instincts. Not nearly as good as OUR parents' parental instincts who MADE us eat the Vienna Sausages and industrial-waste-on-a-shingle.

"Another kid died in China this morning and it was YOUR fault!!!

"And don't forget to drink your glass of sausage gravy. There are kids starving in China. Back when I was a kid, we would have DIED for a glass of sausage gravy!"

"Now hurry up and eat your healthy SPAM, olive loaf, hot dog meatloaf, tuna-potato chip casserole, TV dinner, Wonder bread, bologna, liver sausage, chicken a la king, Velveeta, creamed onions, creamed corn, creamed Brussels sprouts, creamed green beans, creamed lima bean casserole, pigs in a blanket, ("Oh! We would have DIED for pigs in a blanket") dinner…

There are kids STARVING in China!"

CATAPULT QUESTIONS

I recently read (and I'm not making this up) that during the middle ages, dead bodies were sometimes used as catapult ammunition. I guess even back then recycling was a thing. But this brings up a LOT of profound questions:

- What if they shot a little person at you. And the body flew apart during flight and you were killed by an upper body appendage... Would that be SMALL ARMS FIRE?
- How about if they fired your BFF's body at you... Would that be FRIENDLY FIRE?
- Is this where Barnum and Bailey first got the idea for the human cannonball?
- Isn't history strange?

I REALLY wish I had MY very own catapult…
Wouldn't THAT be a great way to take out the garbage?

COULD IT BE?

After my father passed away, I was going through the stuff in his house and I found that my dad had two copies of REMEMBER EVERYTHING YOU READ. Could it be that he bought the first copy…

And then forgot?

CHILDISH PROTECTIVE SERVICES

ME AS A CHILD: Dad, can I pet the nice badger?

DAD: If you can catch it, you can pet it.

CUBAN DISMISSAL CRISIS

Recently, my wife Nancy Matthews and I went to Cuba where we met this guy. His name is Manny—Manny Fofander. He owns and operates an urban sweatshop where he manufactures Crocs footwear knockoffs and sells black-market Toblerones out the back door. He has a wife named Yolander (maiden name Bo'bander) who also lives in Cuba.

Yolander Bo'Bander-Fofander, wife of Manny Fofander, is head of quality assurance for the Fofander Crocs knockoff manufacturing operation and inspects each and every pair of Crocs knockoffs to make sure that they're hideous and tacky enough for export to "the States." If they fail to pass mustard (who doesn't enjoy a good condiment joke now and then?), Yolander Bo'Bander-Fofander sends them back to final assembly where they are lovingly adorned with a chic "camo" motif. She also taste-tests a lot of the Toblerones.

Disclaimer: Some of that might have been made up.

(But we DID go to Cuba.)

It was nice.

CAREER TESTING

When my son, Alex Matthews was in high school, they gave him an official, bona fide CAREER TEST to evaluate his skills in order to help him to choose his life career path. His results were (and I'm not making this up): A) vending machine operator or B) zoo-keeper.

As it turns out, he is currently a happy and successful mechanical engineer and has been for the past few years.

I'd like to point out it may not be inherently obvious, but the official, bona fide CAREER TEST was not a COMPLETE MISFIRE. Because Alex DOES enjoy a fulfilling and gratifying AVOCATION as a vending machine operator—in which he deposits coins into various assorted vending machines and then eats the crap that falls out of them.

CONFOUND INTEREST

Hey! Let's talk about the MAGIC OF COMPOUND INTEREST: Taking into account present interest rates, if you had deposited just A SINGLE ONE-DOLLAR-BILL into a simple passbook savings account during the year of George Washington's inauguration...

You would be dead today.

CONFUSION SAYS

Some people say the glass is half empty.

Others say the glass is half full.

I say: "Leave the bottle."

CROSS TRAINING

Back when I was a kid, there used to be such a thing as a GIRL'S BIKE. Maybe there still is. I don't know.

It was a bike that was designed and built WITHOUT the crossbar. I think the idea was that you could ride one while wearing a dress… or nun's habit… or a hoop skirt, and NOT get wound up in the sprocket. I don't know. I just remember it was nice to ride because, as a boy, when your feet inevitably slipped off the pedals, you didn't end up zesting your lemons on the crossbar like you did on a boy's bike. But that's not the point. HERE'S the point:

If a MAN works out on a GIRLS bike, would that be considered cross-training?

CAST PARTY

I think this would be a cool thing to do if I ever broke an arm:

Instead of having friends sign my cast, I would painstakingly copy all of the signatures off of the Declaration of Independence and sprinkle them all over the cast in a random fashion. I think this would confuse a lot of people…

Because hey! Who knew the founding fathers had Sharpies?

CHILDLESS FATHERS

Do you know why the Catholic church won't allow their priests to marry? I think it might be because they'd probably have WIVES and KIDS.

And then it would be confusing and embarrassing for everyone involved if the priests' wives spent all day yelling at the kids:

"WAIT TILL YOUR FATHER GETS HOME!"

CARPE DIEM!

CARPE DIEM! Seize the day!

Translated from an old Roman text it has become one our leading pop culture motivational clichés. And some days, I HATE it. Some days I just don't wake up with that "seize the day" kind of attitude. Let's face it, some days just turn out to be "pull the covers back over your head and assume the fetal position while appealing to the universe for minimal blanket-puffing-gaseous-discharge-episodes" kind of days.

For these types of days, I've made up my own phrase. I have not had the energy nor discipline to trademark it so feel free to use it when appropriate:

CRAPE DIEM.

(I'll leave you to do the translation for yourself.)

CREATIVITY

One man's CREATIVITY…

Is another man's MENTAL ILLNESS.

CUL DE SAC SMARTS

Everyone talks about BOOK SMARTS or STREET SMARTS and how one might be superior to the other. Well, there's another type of smarts that are seldom talked about. Because, unless you've lived through it like I have—grew up in the suburbs, lived in those tract houses, and walked those grassy, picket-fenced-in lawns—you just won't be able to understand it. Ya. That's right. I'm talking about CUL DE SAC SMARTS. Cul de sac smarts may SEEM like they lead nowhere, but CUL DE SAC SMARTS are the key to survival in the cold-hearted, merciless, suburban savannah.

CUL DE SAC SMARTS say you always carry reserve lunch money so you can still buy lunch after the bully extorts your sacrificial lunch money.

CUL DE SAC SMARTS say you always let the bigger, menacing "jocks" copy off of your physics homework.

And CUL DE SAC SMARTS say, when threatened, you ALWAYS share your Tater Tots.

And the fact is that CU DE SAC SMARTS will beat STREET SMARTS EVERY SINGLE TIME!

Alright… Not EVERY time… Nine-out-of-ten times…

Okay…

Never.

(Pedro for president).

CATHOLIC SCHOOL OF ROCK

Recently, I was having breakfast with a friend and he was recounting stories from his youth—specifically his traumatic Catholic school experiences. During our conversation, as a fortuitous bonus, we happened to create a most-excellent new band name which I now offer to you:

The Violent Nuns

Featuring Sister Mary Elephant.

(With a nod to the Blues Brothers).

CURSIVE! FOILED AGAIN!

Absolutely NO ONE reads cursive writing anymore.

Young people don't know how…

And people my age can't SEE it.

CARPAL TALKING SYNDROME

I wonder if the "All of our operators are busy. Please wait for the next available representative" lady ever gets tired of saying that.

CLAIRE BARE

Shave the cheerleader… shave the world.

(From the Greek TV series Gyros)

CHERRY SMOOTHIE

I was talking to a friend and we were saying that there's nothing better on a cool, crisp, autumn day than a nice refreshing cherry smoothie. So, having said that…

Here's my recipe for the world-famous Bob Matthews Cherry Smoothie:

Take the following ingredients, combine them in a blender and blend:

- Cherries
- Other appropriate smoothie foodstuffs

Feel free to substitute for any of the ingredients.

CHRISTMAS SPECIALS

For optimum efficiency, I have decided to avoid the hassle, expense, and time-wasting of Christmas shopping this year and just encourage my friends to steal office supplies from work.

Take as much as you want! I'm feeling generous this year!

Merry Christmas.

CONFLICT IN Bob's WoRld

I don't want to alarm anyone, but about a week ago…

The voices in my head started an argument and it sounded REALLY BAD! I'm not sure what all the commotion has been about.

Sometimes I wish they spoke English.

CAVY GRAVY

I'd rather have a ham and cheese sandwich than say…

A HAMSTER and cheese sandwich.

But that's just me.

CALLER ID?

So, here's the problem that I have with caller ID:

When I call from any phone that is NOT my own personal phone, my name doesn't come up on the other end and so people don't bother to pick up. And coincidentally, they ALSO don't pick up when I call from my OWN phone. So, tell me…

Where's the advantage?

CLINICALLY DEPRESSED

The sky was clinically depressed that day, my friends…

Like an old man shooing kids off his front lawn.

(With a nod to George Costanza)

CECS

Whenever I fly, I feel like I should be awarded Continuing Education Credits by the airlines for having learned:

A) How to buckle a seat belt and

B) How to pull that dangling yellow oxygen mask… not AWAY from… but TOWARD me.

COMPACT PEN

I have a compact pen. It's pretty unique. It telescopes. You can extend it to use it and squash it to store it away. The bad thing is, the pen is dark BLUE… but the ink is BLACK. So THAT'S confusing…

Did I mention that it telescopes?

People sometimes ask me, "How did you ever FIND something like that?"

Well, it was through a very well-planned, complex, serendipitous, and fortuitous chain of events:

1. I went to Amazon and typed "compact pen" in the search bar.
2. Amazon showed me a normal-sized listing for a compact pen.
3. I gave some—but not ALL—of my money to Amazon in exchange for the compact pen.
4. Using a big, brown truck; Amazon delivered the compact pen right to my house.

(Join me again next week on BOB'S WORLD when we'll learn how to prepare authentic, takeout-like, industrial-grade chicken nuggets from common household ingredients you may already have in your garage.)

"Bad robot!"

CATCH A BUZZ

One of today's trends seems to be vibration. Apparently, if YOU can make it vibrate, WE will buy it.

My wife just bought a four-pack of vibrating toothbrushes. Not electric toothbrushes like a Sonicare or even those disposable Crest spinning electric toothbrushes. But little, ordinary, disposable toothbrushes with vibrating bristles. Oral-B makes them (and is, by the way, ABSOLUTELY FREE to send me money for this artful product placement). Allegedly, the vibrating action removes surface stains. I'll bet they also make your head buzz when you use them.

I already have a vibrating razor. Again, not an electric shaver but a little, ordinary, disposable safety razor with vibrating blades. Gillette makes it and it's probably got around 19 blades all lined up like tiny little Venetian blinds. And you would think if you were going to drag an object with 19 (literally) razor-sharp blades across your soft, vulnerable facial skin; you'd want the whole works to be rock steady to avoid that loose-meat-face effect. But no. They vibrate the heck out of that thing. I like it a lot because it makes my head buzz when I use it.

My smartness phone also vibrates. I carry it in my pocket and when I get a call, it vibrates my butt to alert me. I like that too.

What's next? Vibrating spatulas to loosen those stubborn pancakes? Or vibrating toasters so that if you bought one…

You would have a toaster that vibrates?

How about vibrating shoes? You could have a continuous, never-ending foot massage. And if you're going to vibrate your feet, why not vibrate EVERYTHING. Vibrating clothes. Make your WHOLE OUTFIT vibrate—including your hat. Why not? The only potential problem I can see might come from carrying your smartness phone in your pocket, as I do now. If your phone rang while your clothes were vibrating, and the two vibration systems were out of phase, the phone vibrations might actually CANCEL OUT the pants vibrations and the ONLY WAY YOU'D KNOW YOU'D GOT A PHONE CALL IS IF YOUR BUTT WENT QUIET. I surely wouldn't like THAT.

Other than that (and the fact that you'd ALWAYS look like you were shivering) I think vibrating clothes is a first-rate idea! You'd have a continuous, never-ending full body massage. And that would help ease the anxiety and tension you'd get from listening to that low-grade hum all day emanating from your vibrating clothes.

(I think I like that vibrating hat idea because it'd SURELY make my head buzz when I wore it.)

CINEMANIAC

So, I watched a movie called "300" last night. Here's the gist of what happened:

Some very tall Persian guy delivered a message to "the Spartans." They ("the Spartans") were NOT entirely pleased with the content of the message, so they pushed the Persian guy into a big, deep hole. So now, HE'S dead.

Next, came the standard, obligatory, gratuitous, sex scene (which I couldn't get my DVR going in time for).

Then 300 Spartans took a trip to the seashore on the north of Greece. The guy leading the way played (and I'm definitely NOT making this part up) two flutes AT ONCE!

A million Persians landed in boats and camped on the seashore. (Which had to have caused a MASSIVE sewage problem—but, oddly, [like the big elephant poop in the room] they never addressed this in the movie.)

The million Persians went on to kill a Greek village and, for fun, they stuck everyone up in a tree. It was kind of like a Christmas tree (but with dead people as ornaments).

Then the million Persians tried to kill the 300 Spartans—but the 300 Spartans weren't having it. So they hacked at each other for a while in slow motion.

Unfortunately, some horses were killed—which is a SHAME because no one likes to see horses die (except for that housekeeping lady who made that guy's bed in The Godfather).

After a while, "the Spartans" ended up creating a landfill out of Persians. And "the Spartans" seemed very proud of their accomplishment. "The Persians"—not so much.

Later "the Persians" attacked with a big rhinoceros because what self-respecting army doesn't have a RHINOCEROS? And that didn't work, so they tried ELEPHANTS. And THAT didn't work, so they dug a little deeper into their circus arsenal and brought in the Persian clown car. 750 Persian clowns jumped out of a 1946 Volkswagen Beetle (which was difficult to come by in 480 BCE) and viciously attacked with rubber chickens and big inflatable bats. But sadly for "the Persians" that ALSO didn't work.

Then, Leonidas, King of "the Spartans" made a stirring speech to his men. And he said, "Ready your breakfast and eat hearty. For tonight, WE DINE IN HELL!"

And THAT was when I began to suspect that I had been wrong ALL ALONG.

"300" was MOST DEFINITELY NOT a movie about bowling.

CAPTAIN BEEFHEART

I have a friend who's a little older than me whose heart started doing some sort of gooshy, squirty, fluttery thing. Also, he was tired all the time.

So, he went to see his doctor. And, as it turns out, he had a bad heart valve. I guess it was leaky and it made the blood flow backward through his body or something. So, I guess his doctor politely, compassionately, and tactfully informed him of his options. (In the dialog below, I'm going to refer to my friend as "Bob" because that's what his parents named him.)

DOCTOR: You're gonna have to get that fixed or you're gonna die.
BOB: Wha?
DOCTOR: We're going to put in a new one.
BOB: Where the fuh-HECK are you going to get a NEW heart valve??!!
DOCTOR: From the Human Spare Parts Store, Bob... Ha, ha, ha, Bob... Just a little medical humor there. Actually, Bob, we're going to give you a heart valve from a cow.

Now, between you and me, when I heard this, I was kind of disappointed. I mean, the heart valve from a COW. A CATTLE valve! Seems a little low-tech to me. I was disillusioned.

I mean, I remember several years ago, when my mother-in-law got a hip replacement, she got a very COOL new hip. It was made from titanium. TITANIUM! A shiny, light-weight, incredibly strong, SPACE AGE material. Think of it. TITANIUM! THAT, my friends, is Six-Million-Dollar-Man-stuff! TITANIUM HIPS! She's practically a death-dealing, science-fictiony, cyborg now.

On the other hand, my friend was getting his human spare parts from the same place we get CHEESEBURGERS! I hope they didn't order it off the dollar menu. What's next? Prosthetic limbs from the dollar store?

Anyway, Bob had to stay in the hospital for a week or so. I guess Bob must have had the "good" health insurance because I understand that the "bad" insurance would have made him go through the drive-thru.

So, to wrap up, the operation was successful and my friend Bob is thankfully doing okay. The cow... not so much. I guess when he was discharged, they gave him a little plastic bag with his home care instructions, his medications and...

A Happy Meal toy.

[rimshot]

EPILOGUE: The story above is mostly based on truth. Bob was a real person—a good friend of mine for more than 30 years. As you can tell from the tone of this epilogue, Bob has since passed. At the time of the writing of this post, the operation had already been completed and was wildly successful. They had actually found that they could simply repair his existing heart valve and thus, there had been no need to transplant a cow valve. However, I kept the cow valve in my version because my need for the "cheeseburger joke" overrode my nearly-always-secondary need for journalistic integrity.

Bob died of a heart attack around a year later. Now, I am editing this book and am faced with the decision of keeping this post or eighty-sixing it out of "respect."

Obviously, I'm leaving it in. In MY value system, there's no better way to show respect for someone than to recall funny stories and memories of them (however embellished they may be). His widow has requested that we keep everything (tributes, etc.) "low key." Out of respect for her, I will not mention Bob's last name (even though, in MY value system, it DESERVES mention).

You may disagree with my decisions. It's MY book. I make the final decisions. This may have been the wrong decision—but at least know I didn't make it lightly and that I made it with a good heart.

Miss you Bob.

COMMENTARY CLARITY

I think when the golf announcer says someone drove the ball over 400 yards, I think they should specify WHOSE yards they drove over. They should at least specify the neighborhood. City lots are pretty small, so, you know—not particularly impressed. But if you can hit over 400 yards out in farm country…

Now you've GOT something.

COULD IT BE?

I've noticed that my clothes have been fitting a little more "snug" lately. And also, I've been feeling a little "bloated." I think maybe…

I'm retaining fat.

CHAPTER FOUR
Dogs, Dunkirk, and Dummness

DEADLIEST ICE BUSH CRAB TROOPERS

Cable TV is for the birds. And when I say "the birds" I don't mean those coveted, exalted, majestic Birds-O-Prey (another promising flavor idea Lifesaver should be pursuing) like the eagle, or the condor, or the flying squirrel. I mean significantly less coveted, significantly less exalted, significantly less majestic—let's just say: significantly less significant (how can I put this)—STUPIDER birds. Like the mosquito... or those airborne dust flakes that like to hang out in sunbeams.

But first—a confession:

I have "basic" cable. I didn't pay for ANY upgrades. There... I've SAID it.

So, it's not like I don't know that I've caused most of my cable TV problems myself. I DO know it's my own fault (because I chose not to pay the extra money) that I don't get to watch cool things like "the big game", or first run TV episodes or movies where the ACTUAL MOVIE, not just the commercials, are in color. So, I get that part. I didn't pay for the "premium" stuff. That's not the problem. The problem is that the basic, standard programming… (how to put this delicately?) … SUCKS. The catchphrase for whoever is selecting my cable programming seems to be, "All Alaska—all the time." Or "Alaska—if it's good enough for Sarah Palin, It's good enough for you." Here's a sample of what's on MY cable TV:

Alaska State Troopers: Alaskan police guys approach people's houses and mostly ask, "Hey. What are you doing with that gun?" I guess it's in its billionth season because EVERYONE in Alaska (according to cable TV) seems to own somewhere close to 317 guns (and a LOT of whiskey).

Alaskan Bush People: This show is about a family that goes on a 20-year camping trip and calls it "home."

Ice Road Truckers: These guys drive trucks. Guess where? On ice. That's where. (Talk about an accurately named show).

Bearing Sea Gold: These guys (who seem to have ABSOLUTELY NO IDEA WHAT THEY'RE DOING) look for gold underwater.

Gold Rush: These guys (who ALSO seem to have ABSOLUTELY NO IDEA WHAT THEY'RE DOING) look for gold on land. I think if they combined this show with Bearing Sea Gold; it could air on C-SPAN.

Deadliest Catch: Alaskan crab fishermen, fishing for crab in Alaska, spend the majority of each episode swearing at each other because A) They're not catching any crab, or B) They're "on the crab."

I guess if I was "on the crab" I'd swear too.

DANGST

I feel like deep, down inside, everyone is insecure.

And those of us who go through life performing with apparent confidence are simply the ones who feel most SECURE with our own insecurity.

DUNKIRK

The missus and I just returned from seeing Dunkirk (the movie, NOT the actual French seaport).

SPOILER ALERT…

It's a story about boating.

DOGS AND CATS… REIGNING TOGETHER

When there's a huge downpour, we say IT'S RAINING CATS AND DOGS. So, when there's a slight sprinkle, why don't we say:

IT'S DRIZZLING KITTENS AND PUPPIES?

(Am I the only one THIMKING?)

DIET CONFUSION

When I was a kid, we ate the foods that our parents gave us (which were EXACTLY the same foods their parents gave them). However, in the 1970's, ALL that changed. That's when the "EXPERTS" starting getting involved.

In the 70's, America went on a low-fat, low-flavor, high-sugar diet. But that just ACCELERATED the problem and we all got FATTER. So, we switched to Robert Atkins' high-protein, high-fat, high-flavor diet—and we LOVED it—until we all CONTINUED to get fatter (and sicker) AND Dr. Robert Atkins DIED of a heart attack.

Then we were counseled to eat like cavemen—because why NOT eat the diet that people with an average life-expectancy of ALMOST THIRTY-YEARS used to eat?

We even had the good old U.S. of A. government advising us: We had the Food Wheel, the Food Pyramid, the Food Plate, the Food Pie Chart, the Pie Food Chart, The Pie vs. Food Chart, and various other food-industry sponsored guidelines.

Now we have vegan diets, wheat-belly diets, whole-food-plant-based diets, Keto diets, Kryptonite diets, yada, yada, yada…

It's gotten SO confusing…

I don't know WHICH DIET I should be cheating on anymore!

DEPP THOUGHTS

Johnny Depp claims to be part Native American by way of his great-grandmother. So, I think a good Native American name for Johnny Depp would be:

Edward Runs-with-Scissorhands. Or… How about…

DANCES WITH SCISSORS?

DEACON BLOBS

As I look at the opening line of Steely Dan's 1970's hit song, Deacon Blues;

I gotta wonder if they might have written it on Thanksgiving Day—right after finishing dinner.

(Go ahead. Google it. It'll be worth it.)

DISORDERLY

It seems to me some of the psychological folks might have had a little trouble in naming some of their disorders. Those of you who know me, know I'm always willing to help. So, here's just a few suggestions:

Firstly, I think that OCD (Obsessive Compulsive Disorder) people should instead be labeled OCO people because the fact is, they are not DISorderly. They are obsessively and compulsively ORDERLY.

Secondly, I also think that if people with eating disorders who lose weight by throwing up are labeled as having bulimia, people with eating disorders who lose weight by taking laxatives should be labeled as having POOlimia.

Thirdly and lastly, the fear of phobias is labeled PHOBOPHOBIA, and for the record…

That one's a keeper.

DO YOU MIND?

I read that the Navy SEALs have a certain empowering mindset that is taught to them and vigorously trained into them.

They are taught that whenever they feel they are totally spent, exhausted, drained, and burned out—when they feel as if they are dead on their feet and they can't go on—they are, in actuality, still at 40%. FORTY PERCENT!!! In other words: when you feel as if you're absolutely DONE and you can no longer go on, in reality, you've only used up 60% of your resources. You've still got 40% left "in the tank."

This means that the next time you see some pro athlete or coach on TV and they stare right into the camera and tell all of us out here in TV-Land that "the team gave 110%"; unless all their teammates were ex-Navy SEALs, they actually only gave 40% of 110%. That's LESS THAN HALF of their efforts.

Lazy prima donna bastards.

DISMANTLED

There's a whole heck-of-a-lot-o-stuff that we, the human racers, don't know. Way, way back during the early-evil times and ESPECIALLY during the mid-evil times; we didn't know even MORE of a whole heck-of-a-lot-o-stuff. But then, during the late-evil times (also sometimes called "The Renaissance"), Sir Cam Newton Da Vinci invented science and we, the human racers, began to figure out stuff. For instance, simple-minded mid-evil surfs, pheasants and gnarlets believed that their TV sets were powered by magical devil-bunnies. But then they were shown by science (in the form of Bill Nye) that their TVs were actually powered by little subatomic particles called protons and electrocutions moving rapidly through wires and electronic components such as inductors, resistors, transgenders, and decapitators. That was yesteryear. Fast-forward a whole heck-of-a-lot-o-years to today.

So, for us, the human racers, science has turned out to be both a boon and a not-so-much. For instance, we have now learned to split the atom. This is a good thing, just in case someone is making something and they don't need the WHOLE atom—just part of an atom—we can DO that. But it's also a bad thing in that atom-splitting has given us the power to destroy the planet 921 MILLION times over. And being able to destroy the planet 921 MILLION times over is a great power. And, as the old saying goes: With great power comes great POWER CHORDS. But that's not my point.

International scientists are planning a really big-deal digging party. They are planning to drill into the earth's mantle. The mantle is the part of the earth right beneath the crust and it makes up about 90 percent of the mass of our planet. (Think of it as the earth's chewy liquid center.) Anyway, as I said in the beginning, there's a whole heck-of-a-lot-o-stuff that we, the human racers, don't know. And one of the things the international scientists admitted to not knowing is the exact composition of the mantle.

"We don't know the exact composition of the mantle yet," said international researcher Natsue Abe.

So, I maintain, that if these international so-called scientists don't know the exact composition of the mantle, they won't know what will happen if they puncture the crust and drill into it. I don't know much about the mantle either, but I DO know volcanoes and fumaroles come out of it. And I also read that the Yellowstone National Park area of the mantle has the power to destroy the planet 921 MILLION times over. So, my fear is that if these international so-called scientists puncture the crust, 90 percent of the earth's mass might come squirting out of that hole, looking like an uncontrolled high-pressure fire hose. And our planet, along with we human racers, could go erratically shooting around our general galaxy area like an untied balloon being spastically propelled around the room by its jet-nozzle blast at some kind of cosmic birthday party…

And then wouldn't WE be the laughing stock of the Universe!

DIDN'T QUITE MEASURE UP

My father was sort of a particular and conservative man. "Measure twice—cut once," my dad always said. And so, that advice became kind of ingrained into me—to the point that now I always do that. I measure once and mark it. And then I ALWAYS measure a second time before cutting. But it's at this point that his instructions seem to get a little vague and confusing to me.

I never know whether to make my cut at the FIRST mark I made or at the SECOND—so I always split the difference. So THAT seems to make sense. But here's the problem:

Nothing EVER seems to fit right.

I'm not so sure Dad knew what he was doing.

DON'T LOOK UP!

I think the movie King Kong has been remade about 160 times (although I've only seen three versions). Each time they do a remake, cinematic technology gets a little better and this allows them to make Kong seem a little more terrifying. But here's the thing: even though they follow Kong around for HOUR AFTER HOUR, there's one terrifying thing that, for sure, you'd think you'd see—but you NEVER do. You never see King Kong poop.

Now THAT would be terrifying.

PLOP! CRUNCH!

"OH, THE POOMANITY!"

DANGER CLOSE!

We humans are deathly afraid of lions, tigers, bears (oh my!), sharks, spiders, Uzi-wielding chimps, Godzilla—animals like that. But THOSE ANIMALS ARE NOT THE REAL DANGER. Let me repeat that:

THOSE ENEMAS SQUARE KNOT THE WIFFLE FLANGER.

(Sorry. My "paste" key has been "on the Fritz" lately.)

Okay. But, here's my point: Do you know who the most dangerous animals REALLY are? Dogs. That's right. Dogs. Here's why:

Dogs are like the black ops, special forces of the animal kingdom. That's right. They are the infiltrators—the clandestine, behind-the-lines, paws-on-the-ground, special operatives who have infiltrated our lives, homes, and hearts. Just like those Mata Hari type of seductive, undercover, female-type, sex-oozing spies who seduced and wormed their way into the hearts (and beds) of World War I high-command officers in order to gain classified, hush-hush, top-secret secrets; the dogs in our lives lick our faces and pee on our floors—all the time gathering intelligence. (Okay. Not QUITE the same, but you get my drifting.)

Isn't it ODD that dogs are ALWAYS watching? When we eat, they sit and stare at us. When we leave the house, they follow us RIGHT TO THE DOOR—ALWAYS watching closely. When we're outside, they keep an eye on our EVERY MOVE through the window. When we come back home—THERE THEY ARE! RIGHT AT THE DOOR! Waiting. Staring. ALWAYS WATCHING! When we come out of the bathroom, there they are—RIGHT AT THE DOOR! AGAIN, with the waiting and staring. It makes you wonder: Were they out there peeking under the door at us while we were in there "doing our BUSINESS"? No way to tell. But I'll just BET they WERE! Because that's their job.

And people always wonder: What does my dog DO all day long when I'm at work.

I think they spend most of the day snooping through our important papers, writing field reports, and sending coded messages back to the Kanine Hoch Kommand—communicating in Morse Code with their squeaky toys and their secret, hidden radio transmitters. And then—they use any available spare time to pee on our floors, poop on our carpets and maybe, shred the occasional throw pillow—in order to MAINTAIN THEIR COVER.

So, PROTECT YOURSELF.

Remember: "Forewarned is fore-told-about." Don't turn your back on your dog—ANY dog—even for a moment. They are canine BACK-STABBERS! (Metaphorically speaking, that is—because they don't actually HAVE that opposable-thumb-thingy you need to hold a knife).

So, I guess, in reality—they would be—NOT back-stabbers—but "butt-biters." Ya. BUTT-BITERS. (Except for those little ankle-biters.) But don't turn your back on those little ankle-biters either, because, at heart, those little ankle-biters are big butt biter wannabes. (That's BIG butt-biter-wannabes—not BIG-BUTT biter-wannabes [just to be clear that even SMALL human butts are "up for grabs", so to speak]).

But the ACTUAL point is: Dogs are dangerous. They are a serious threat to our personal people species. Believe me. They're in deep cover, waiting and gathering information. Sure, they look cute. They look friendly. But NEVER FORGET that they are SPIES. They are AGENTS. They are SPOOKS. They are MOLES. Okay, maybe not moles… because that's a COMPLETELY DIFFERENT species.

And THEY (the moles) are OKAY with me—because, unlike dogs—THEY (the moles) are NOT planning to kill off all the humans and take over the world. And, in MY book… that's DEFINITELY a plus.

And ANOTHER thing…

I don't like the way those TROPICAL FISH have been staring at me lately…

DON'T DO THIS

If a bat ever gets loose in your house, don't chase it around all over and try to kill it with a hammer. Because I can tell you…

That gets expensive REAL quick.

DIPLOMACY 101: SPACE GUYS

I think if aliens ever invaded our planet and they had those huge, soft, mushy heads—like the ones you see in those SiFi movies that look like someone took a large intestine, put some eyeballs on it, and stuck it on a stick-figure-body with ribs; I think, as a friendly gesture, we should hold them down and put those big football helmets on them—the ones with that key-lock on the strap that keeps that helmet from falling off during any sort of vigorous activity. Then maybe smack them in the head a few times with a large pipe or a hammer or something to show them how the helmets would protect them from getting intestinal-head injuries.

Maybe then, they'd see how peaceful we were and wouldn't destroy our planet after all.

DSM-5

What's the difference between a psychopath and a sociopath?

(Asking for a friend.)

DUMMNESS

Just to show you how dumb CERTAIN SPOUSES can be around my house:

Who was that guy that lost all his strength when that woman cut off his hair? My silly wife thinks it was SAMSON. Can you BELIEVE it? Samson! Should have seen her face when I reminded her it was CARROT TOP.

And that's just ONE example.

CHAPTER FIVE
Economics, Entomology, and Empty Nesters

EXPERIENCE

Now HERE'S something I've had to learn the hard way:

Those voices in your head? That constant, relentless, NEVER-ENDING chatter? Whispering, demanding, SCREAMING! TELLING YOU WHAT TO DO!

It's not ALWAYS the best advice.

EMPTY NESTERS

I guess my wife and I now have what's called empty nest syndrome. Both our kids Alex and Kristen have metaphorically "flown the coop" but have left a good portion of their stuff behind. So technically, our nest isn't ACTUALLY empty because it's still full of "kid droppings."

But now they've both grown up and left. I miss them and am sad that they're gone. But I am glad that they've grown up. Because as little kids, they really scared "the bejesus" out of me. I was there for both of their births. I watched them come out. Some of you fathers have been through this and I'm sure you'll agree. It's just like that scene from that ALIEN movie where that THING rips its way out of that guy's chest just as easily as you or I might poke our fingers through a day-old pudding skin. That alien thing pops out, takes a quick look around, gargles a couple of things in alien baby-talk (which only sounds like panda farts to my uneducated ear) and scoots across the room like a startled cockroach running for cover under your refrigerator.

Alex was my first born. When we brought him home, I was terrified. Every time I walked past his crib, I was afraid he was going to burst through those bars, fly across the room, latch onto my face and stick some sort of alien tentacle, probe, appendage, endoscope, peashooter THING down my throat and implant a little alien fetus thing that would one day mature and come blasting, billowing, bursting forth with the power of ten billion butterfly sneezes (Moody Blues reference—Google it) through MY poor thoracic "pudding skin"—thus, completing the evil alien monster CIRCLE OF LIFE. Hakuna Matata… NOT!

About the time I'm starting to relax just a little, my wife drags me back to the hospital for another one of these alleged "births." And another one of these little alien life forms comes bursting and sneezing out of her belly. And NOW, I've got TWO of them in the house! (By the way: When I say "NOW", I mean "then").

So ya, that was 20-some odd years ago. But I AM glad they've grown up and are adults now. Why? Because:

A) The panda fart noises have mostly subsided and…

B) They've gotten WAY too big to latch onto my face.

ENOUGH!

Everyone says to follow your dreams. Well, I've had about ENOUGH of that.

Let my dreams follow ME for once…

See how THEY like it.

ECHO DRIVE

Most of you know, I've got an Amazon Echo—one of those voice command computer thingys that you yell voice commands at. Owning Alexa (that's what I've named her) has opened my eyes to an amazing fact. In many of the futuristic spaceship movies that I watched, many of the futuristic spaceships ALSO have Amazon Echoes in them! I know this because I keep seeing the futuristic spaceship captains yelling stuff at their voice command futuristic spaceship computers like:

"Computer! Bring us to heading two-niner-oner! Computer! Set laser printers to STUN!"

So, being the incredibly intellectual giant that I are, it suddenly occurred to me that since I've installed Alexa in my house (just like the futuristic spaceships) I SHOULD BE ABLE TO DRIVE MY HOUSE AROUND WITH VOICE COMMANDS (just like the futuristic spaceships)—maybe even at WARP SPEED (just like the futuristic spaceships)—although it didn't mention anything about this on the tiny, cheesy Amazon Echo instruction card that came in the box with "the unit."

ME: Alexa, come to cruising speed.
ALEXA: Hmmm. I don't know that.
ME: Alexa, fire plasma torpedoes one and two!
ALEXA: Hmmm. I don't know that.

[Me getting frustrated]

ME: Alexa! set a course for the Byzantine Empire!
ALEXA: Hmmm. I don't know that one.
ME: Open the pod bay doors please HAL.
ALEXA: I'm sorry Dave, I'm afraid I can't do that.

[Me getting agitated. Picking up a hammer.]

ME: ALEXA! PLAY MASTER OF PUPPETS!

ALEXA: Bump! ... Bum, Bum, BUMMMMM...

ME: This thing is AMAZING!

EXCERPT FROM MARTHA STEWART BATHROOM LIVING:

To ensure effortless and efficacious dispensing, when installing a new roll of toilet paper, the free end should ALWAYS be fed over the top.

Encountering a previously installed roll with the end protruding from underneath is a telltale sign that you are most certainly dealing with a low-class pooper.

(Thank you, Martha.)

EGOOCEROUS

You know how we all have that innate tendency to try and make ourselves feel superior? How we're always mentally comparing ourselves to others—always looking for areas in which we fare better than they do?

Are we the only species that does that? For instance, I wonder if rhinos don't sometimes look at hippos and think to themselves…

"Boy, HE'S really let himself go."

ENTOMOLOGY QUESTIONS

Do ants ever get humans in their pants? How would that work?

Discuss.

ECONOMICS GUY

Admittedly, I don't know much about economics, but I DO know a thing or two about personal finance.

For instance, I recently bought a package of three telescoping back-scratchers for eleven dollars. A single telescoping back-scratcher would have cost me five dollars. So, buying THREE of them for eleven dollars was clearly a very GOOD deal and a WISE personal finance decision. Now, of course, you might say, "You hardly ever use a back-scratcher and you have only one back so why would you EVER need more than one? WHY BUY THREE? It seems like a waste."

And I might reply, "I got three telescoping back-scratchers for eleven dollars.

"That seems PRETTY GOOD for someone who doesn't know much about economics!"

EXPEDIENTNESS?

Lately, I've been trying to figure out ways to get faster at writing these posts. And after careful analysis of my process…

I find that it's a LOT more expedienter if I don't waste time looking up stuff in the dictionary.

CHAPTER SIX
Friends, Fish, and Facebook

FLOATING WITH THE OLDIES

When I was young, I used to hate going on vacation with older people. Now that I have become "muddle-aged", I have become more tolerant of traveling with old people—and when I say "old", I mean "my age." So, eight of us old timers decided to take a vacation together in Florida because it appears that it's the only place people our age are allowed to go. And when I say eight of us went, I mean the four wives went and lugged their "devoted" husbands along with them in an affiliation that social scientists refer to as a "symbiotic relationship." In this arrangement, the men are required to schlep around absolutely EVERYTHING the couple owns—except for their own personal travel documents.

It seems that the MEN of "our age" are unable to hang on to our own personal travel documents while simultaneously performing ANY other complex task such as going to the bathroom (according to the WOMEN of "our age"). I know my own particular wife seems to think that I cannot be trusted to wander around unsupervised with my own travel documents for fear that either the documents or myself will spontaneously combust and unintentionally destroy a historical monument, set fire to a school bus, or (HEAVEN FORBID) scorch her LUGGAGE (which I would, of course, be carrying). So, we men carry 280-lb suitcases containing our wives' complete summer wardrobes, enough makeup to repaint the USS Nimitz, and two-thirds of their winter wardrobes just in case the next ice age happens to descend upon Florida during the EXACT week that our wives would NOT have unrestricted access to their own residential walk-in closets. In return, symbiotically speaking, the wives carry our travel documents for us in purses in which they have not been able to actually LOCATE anything since the Regan administration.

The first thing we did upon arriving was to go "grocery shopping" which is just a cute little name the wives assigned to this activity because it actually had very little to do with actual groceries. Our purchases consisted of approximately $385 worth of "adult beverages" and some cheese. The cheese was mostly to keep the bottles from clanking together.

One night, after we had just finished drinking dinner and were settling in for after-dinner drinks, someone suggested that we should "go somewhere" and "do something." So, accordingly, in our dinner-induced brain-states, we took a poll and decided that functionally and physically, we were all approximately 37 years younger than our birth certificates would lead one to believe. We settled on renting Jet Skis. The plan was "the men" would sit in front and expertly pilot the personal watercrafts and "the women" would sit in back and do their best to survive the men's attempts at expertly piloting the personal watercrafts.

Let me begin by saying my wife is not really an "outdoorsy person." And I say that in the same way that I might mention that the Pope won't be playing professional football this Sunday. Now don't get me wrong. My wife actually LOVES the outdoors. She often likes to look at it from inside our car. But she was very quick to notice that the Jet Ski did not appear to be nearly as weatherproof as our car's passenger compartment—meaning that she might actually have to TOUCH the outdoors during the process of loving it. I took a close look at the Jet Ski thingy and allayed my wife's fears by instantaneously announcing semi-confidently, "I can probably figure this thing out."

Now, I like to think of our particular group as being a group of highly performing people. We have scientists, engineers, policemen, nurses, etc. in our group. So of course, the first thing we did was run into each other and launch my wife—our least water-resistant person—directly into the Gulf of Mexico.

I'd like to point out that the watercraft collision was completely and totally NOT MY FAULT as I was not even driving at the moment of the crash. (I was just sitting in the pilot seat, drifting around, and trying to get my hand untangled from that pesky string in my bathing suit.)

After we got my wife safely (haha) back on the Jet Ski, our guide, Joey, formed us into a single-file line behind him and we headed off (God knows why) out into the ocean. Joey mashed down all the way on that throttle and so did we. And there we were, skimming across the water at over 50 mph—engines roaring in the morning stillness, hydro-rooster tails shooting high into the air, old people skin flapping in the wind. GOD, it was beautiful!

At one point, Joey stopped the whole procession to let a pod of dolphins get a good look at us. They swam around us making a bunch of Flipper-TV-dolphin noises. Joey tried to tell us they were communicating but I think they were just chuckling. I suspect that Joey had a clandestine deal with the dolphins in which he brought them crazy old people perched on Jet Skis so that they (the dolphins) could OBSERVE OUR BEHAVIOR—and, in return, they (also the dolphins) gave him fish. But that's just a theory.

After this; Joey, being the expert guide that he was, showed us a lot more water and some trees at about 200 miles-per-hour.

Then the time came to dismount and turn our Jet Skis in forever. I lamented to myself that this might be my last chance to ever "do a donut" on a personal watercraft. I was concerned that if I consulted with my wife about the feasibility of doing a donut, she might think I was talking about some type of round breakfast pastry. So solely to save her the annoyance of this needless conversation, I figured we'd save time by invoking the Nike mantra to "Just Do It."

Even though, as I said earlier, my wife is NOT crazy about being in the water; after my donut turned out to be a "dunkin donut", she refused to get back OUT of the water while I was still expertly piloting the personal watercraft.

"I'M NOT GETTING BACK ON THAT THING! I'LL WALK IN!" she said lovingly.

As I review the day, I think it's quite funny that the person who least liked the water was the one that fell in the most. Others in my immediate family disagreed with me and told me as much.

When we were done, and relatively safe on the beach, Joey took us aside in a little old-people's circle and gave us a speech. He was actually very complimentary to our group. He said, in the past, he had guided many other groups "of our demographic." And he said it's very typical for people "of our demographic" to lose items in the water: sunglasses… keys… artificial hip replacements… their lives. Joey told us that he was very proud of us because we had only lost some of these things.

Next year, after "grocery shopping", we are planning on looking at the ocean from inside our cars.

FACEBOOK OPERATIONALIZATION QUESTION

I have a technical question that maybe one of you long-time Facebookers can help me with.

I got a message ON my Facebook, FROM Facebook yesterday that said "Congratulations" (implied), "You shared 22 days in a row." I thought to myself, 22 days—that's pretty good—nearly THREE WEEKS! That means I'm starting to get a few things out there, getting my stuff read, getting my opinions heard. So, I decided to do kind of a personal quality review. You know, look back through my past posts with a critical and discerning eye. Examine the things I've written, the issues I've raised... summarize for myself exactly what I've contributed to the Facebook community. So, after doing a review of my past posts… I was wondering…

Is there ANY way for me to unfriend myself?

FRIENDS

I've noticed that since I've made a Facebook and started sharing my ideas regularly, my relationships with the people I deal with face-to-face have radically improved. When we meet, they often kid me with little quips and jokes... especially "What's WRONG with you?!!", "Stop that!" and "Get the hell outta here!" kinda jokes.

My friends are SO supportive.

FAQ

I've had a Facebook now for nearly a couple of months. During that time, I've watched my popularity skyrocket. (Here's a public shout-out to BOTH my followers).

With fame comes a responsibility to MY FANS. I've found that when you're in the public eye such as I am, it becomes more difficult to maintain a private side to life (because of THE FANS). I find that MY FANS are not content with just the small bits of my life that I feed them on Facebook. I've been deluged with questions lately from MY FANS and thought I'd take this time to answer a few representative queries from MY FANS:

Q: Bob, your posts are extremely "unique." Where do you get all your ideas?
A: I get my ideas the same place I get my "facts." I make them up.

Q: I've been following you on Facebook. Does insanity run in your family?
A: Like water. Rapidly downhill—all the way to the sea.

Q: Have you had a stroke?
A: No. My health is fine. Thank you for your concern.

Q: Bob, just what exactly is WRONG with you?
A: Okay… that's enough Q&A for one day.

FILOSOFICAL KWESTION

Suppose there was a planet that had no atmosphere. Also, pretend that there's a tree on this planet. And that this tree topples over (maybe BECAUSE there's no atmosphere) and it makes no sound (ALSO because there's no atmosphere).

Here's what I'm getting at:

If a tree falls down on a gasless planet, and there's no one around to NOT hear it, does it still NOT make a sound?

Discuss.

FUNDUE

The United States of America is often referred to as a MELTING POT—which you Boomers will remember was a popular "dinner party" fad for a total of about 15 minutes back in "the 70s." Now some of you people from "the 70's" may not specifically remember melting pots only because we REALLY "cool" people didn't call them "melting pots." We referred to these artifacts by their snotty French name: "fondue" (from the French "to scald with arrogance"). Here's how they worked:

Ignoring the past 10,000 years or so of human culinary technological progress, we "cool" people elected to eschew all existing cooking paraphernalia such as the stove, the spatula, the coffee masher, and the miter box and just boil some cheese in a bowl with a candle. To begin with, we "cool" people would chop up some processed-cheese-food into lumps and toss them into one of these fondue pots. Next, we'd set the fondue pot on the living room floor on a tall, narrow, unstable iron rack over an open flame and wait for temperatures to reach the "blistering point." Then we'd all sit in a tight circle on the orange shag carpeting around this rickety, medieval-looking, flaming device and drink loads of alcoholic beverages.

After the requisite number of second-degree burns had been accrued, we "cool" people would take tiny food items such as tiny lumps of meat, bread, vegetables, plastic, rubber bands, cat hair, etc. and jam them on the end of pointy, little twig-like forked weapons of mass indigestion. Then we would plunge the tiny food morsels into the melted cheese and leave them in there, submerged—sometimes for HOURS until the tiny food morsels remained THOROUGHLY uncooked. (Just because you BELIEVE you can cook an entire dinner party meal over a birthday candle doesn't mean you CAN cook an entire dinner party meal over a birthday candle.)

Finally, after the sufficient number of alcoholic beverages had been consumed, we'd order pizza.

In the morning, after a good night's sleep; the fondue hostess would arise, cover the burn holes with a throw rug, feed the tiny, raw food morsels to the neighbor's cat, and throw the fondue pot in the trash.

Ahhh… the 70's. They don't make 'em like that anymore.

FLYING TOO CLOSE TO THE SUN

Okay. See if this makes sense to you:

My wife Nancy Matthews and I hopped on a plane and flew about 16 HUNDRED miles to a tiny Caribbean island so we could be burned by a flaming, thermonuclear, celestial object that's 93 MILLION miles away.

(THEN, upon arrival; we smeared a thin, 0.003 mm film of translucent liquid on our skin in order to PROTECT ourselves from the scorching.)

Hoomans.

FLYING CRAB

I'm sitting here in an airplane aisle seat where some guy just bumped me with his butt while getting something down from the overhead bin. Now I want him to die and eternally burn in hell!

(Sometimes traveling makes me cranky.)

FAILURE IS A DEFINITE OPTION

DO NOT BE AFRAID TO FAIL!

Be afraid that you're TOTALLY SURROUNDED by people who have ALREADY failed. And now they're running around, at large in society, free and unsupervised, and exercising all the privileges afforded by an adult ID.

FLYING LESSONS

As I'm writing this, I'm sitting on an airliner. The flight attendant has just, with great aplomb and earnestness, taught us how to use a seat belt. (Not individually, I might add—but in a group lesson).

Next, I've heard we're going to learn how to sip BOILING HOT LIQUIDS from tiny disposable plastic vessels—while we HURTLE THROUGH RAREFIED, HIGH-ALTITUDE, POTENTIALLY-TURBULENT AIR at EXTREMELY high rates of speed!

Seems like a big step.

FISH STORY

Say you're an emu…

???…

No, wait. That's not right.

I'm going to start over…

Say you're a FISH. Ya… That's right… A fish. And you're in a room, under the sea. Maybe like a room in Sponge Bob's house—but NOT a pineapple room—a REAL room made out of waterproof drywall—under the sea. And say you're in a room with a bunch of other fish—a LOT of other fish. But not TOO many other fish. NOT like a whole GAGGLE of fish. Less than a gaggle. But more than "a few."

So, say you're in a room, under the sea, with JUST THE RIGHT AMOUNT of fish. And you gaze around the room admiring everyone's beautiful, healthy-looking, rough, scaly fish skin; UNTIL you spot a little Blue Gill over in the corner who's obviously very shy. And as you look closer, you realize she's feeling self-conscious because she has a case of fish-psoriasis and some of her skin is silky smooth. And it's PAINFULLY OBVIOUS to everyone in this undersea room that EVERYONE HAS NOTICED that she has a VERY BAD case of fish-psoriasis because she has A LARGE NUMBER of large, unsightly, silky smooth patches ALL OVER her body. And even though you're in a room with a bunch of other fish, no one says ANYTHING to ANYONE about it. Certainly, there is much eye contact being made in the room and many of the fish exchange knowing looks. But no one broaches the subject. No one AT ALL.

I guess you could say it was the WHALE in the room. Bahahahaha!!!

The WHALE IN THE ROOM!!! Bahahahahahah. Ha.

Okay. Maybe it needs some work.

FISH BRITCHES

What if you put pants on a fish? What would that look like?

(Stay with me here, because I AM going somewhere with this.)

Imagine, if you were going to put pants on a fish. You'd want them to fit correctly so you'd make them so that they were shaped EXACTLY like its own tail fin. So, if you imagine a fish wearing pants that were shaped EXACTLY like its own tail fin, it would look like a little mermaid (not THE Little Mermaid—A little mermaid). Except it would still have a fish head and a fish body. And since those are the very EXACT things that make a mermaid look like a mermaid; it would literally, look EXACTLY nothing like a mermaid. In fact, if you examined it closely, it would look like… well…

It would look like a fish wearing pants.

(I'm not sure WHERE I'm going with this.)

FAD PRODUCT

I've invented a new and exciting fad product. It's for those times when you wake up and you need a shower, but you're also hungry. On those days, don't you sometimes almost wish you could eat something AND shower… AT THE SAME TIME? Well now, thanks to my new and exciting product, YOU CAN. It's a little innovative product I like to call:

Toast on a Rope.

(Note: Early marketing tests have indicated that this product should NOT be used in the shower with jelly.)

FOAMY POEMY

Isn't technology grand? Also, the internet—that's grand too. Although, technically speaking, I think the internet is actually a PART of technology. And the fact that the internet is actually a part of technology, is ALSO grand.

Anyway, I thought I'd try employing technology (in the form of the internet) to my advantage—to EVERYONE'S advantage, in fact. I thought I'd try a little experiment and use the internet to write a poem. Because the fact is, I'm pretty much unable to write a poem on my own. I write poetry about as well as bears ride bicycles. Sure—they can be TRAINED to ride bicycles. And that can be interesting to watch—at least the first time. But they never really ever get GOOD at it, do they? I mean there's probably a very LOW probability that the Tour de France is going to be won by a circus bear anytime soon. If nothing else, they'd probably get distracted by that squeezy water bottle thing halfway through the race. And before you could say "Bob's your uncle," there's be fountains of water everywhere and some giant, bulky, furry, growling, woodland beast wobbling all over the road, knocking over other world-class cyclists, crashing into the crowd, and chowing down on random fleeing, screaming, terror-stricken spectators.

So, I Googled "poem generator" on the internet which, astonishingly, lead me to a poem generator site. The way it works is you put in a few seed words to get it started and it writes you a poem. I was feeling particularly poetic on that fine day, so I chose the words “foamy”, “flatulent”, “asshat”, and some other descriptive word-seeds and clicked the START button to get it going.

Well, I've got to say, for something as intelligent as the internet, I expected some better poetry than I got. The poem it initially spewed out did not meet my high and lofty poetic poetry poem standards. However, unwilling to accept defeat, I opted to rework the dreadfully trite, synthetic robo-poem by hand. What follows is my poem-writing collaboration WITH the internet. And the result was pretty good I think—MUCH better than any circus bear could have written:

THE TALL AND FOAMY ASSHAT
A poem by The Internet and Bob Matthews

Whose asshat is that? I think I know.
Its owner is quite gassy though.
With asshat shrouding him from head to toe,
I hear methane toots. I cry, “HELLO!”

He gives his asshat a shake,
And screams to me, “MY BUTTOCKS ACHE!”
The only other sound's the break,
Of flatulent wind and then, birds awake.

The asshat is tall, bulbous and proud,
And his breaking wind yet foamy and loud.
Tormented by his bladder, he never sleeps.
Waking up frequently to discharge his peeps.

He rises from his cursed bed,
With thoughts of tinkling in his head,
Donning slippers, trudges he to the head.
Farts fill his asshat. He returns to bed.

(With thanks to the poet, Robert Frost, for the underlying structure.)

FOOL ME ONCE

Fool me once, shame on you.
Fool me twice, shame on you AGAIN!
Fool me three times, SHAME ON YOU THREE TIMES!

Hey! BRING IT ON FOOL!

I can do this ALL DAY.

F(RUIT)=MG

One fine day in 1666, Sir Isaac Newton sat quietly in his mother's garden in Lincolnshire, England. An apocryphal legend has it that an apple fell and bonked him on the head. But, in reality, most believe that he simply witnessed an apple fall harmlessly to the ground. Nevertheless, he drew an insightful analogy between objects always falling (being drawn toward) the center of the earth and the moon unalterably circling (being drawn toward) the center of the earth. And it was ultimately from this line of thought, that he developed his law of universal gravitation—the law that governs the motion of ALL HEAVENLY BODIES.

So what epic thing have YOU accomplished lately with YOUR fruit?

Hmmm?

FOOD NETWORK

If I was head of the Food Network, I'd have my guys whip up some new and yummy Salmonella recipes.

It seems to be getting VERY trendy lately.

("Be sure to try the Sockeye Salmonella. After dinner, you AND it will both be 'planked'.")

FIRST IMPRESSIONS

People seem to instantly like other people who are helpful—who are willing to "chip in", "pull their weight", and "do their share."

So, here's a REALLY GOOD IDEA for when you meet someone new and they invite you over to their house. The very FIRST thing you should do when you arrive is go around to all the rooms, empty all the wastebaskets and take out the trash. (Don't forget to check under the kitchen sink).

You'll be SURPRISED at how much of an impression this little gesture will make.

FUN GRANDPA

I can't wait to have grandchildren—because: baby teeth.

It's gonna be GREAT when one of the grandkids' baby teeth falls out and they put it under their pillow for the tooth fairy. Because then, I'M going to sneak into their room in the middle of the night, pocket the tooth, and replace it with MY DENTURES.

Won't THAT be fun?!!

(Note to self: gotta get some dentures… Oooooo! And a glass eye!!!)

FUN IN THE SAND

I remember one day, when I was still a youngster, mom and I decided it would be “a hoot” to bury dad in the sand. I'm not so sure that dad especially LIKED that idea. But it didn't really matter to mom and I. We just went ahead and did it without even asking his permission. We threw handful after handful of sand on him. And things became so much MORE of “a hoot” after we got in a rhythm. Mom would toss a handful. Then I would throw a handful. Then she would fling another. And before you knew it, good old dad had a big old pile of sand on him!

And the cool thing was, no one EVER found him.

I'll bet his body is STILL buried out there in that desert.

FIRST IRRESPONDER

If a plane ever crashes near my house, I'm going to run over there real quick so I can get there before the NTSB arrives to investigate. Then I'm gonna root around until I find that “Black Box” thingy and I'm going to REPLACE it with a SHOEBOX that I had previously painted black just for this sort of situation.

Then I'm going to hide behind a tree with the REAL “Black Box” and watch what happens next.

So, if you ever hear of a plane crashing near my house, look for ME that evening on the TV!

CHAPTER SEVEN
Graham Crackers, Gulfing, and GPS

GRAHAM CRACKERS? YES. COOKIES? NOT YET.

When I was your age, Alexander Graham Bell hadn't even invented the Internet yet.

GREATEST SALES PITCHES OF ALL TIME... 10,000 BCE: THE FIRST LOBSTER MEAL

[Ogg, a late Cenozoic Era man, offering up a fidgety, wriggling, snapping marine crustacean to his friend, Grog.]

OGG: "Here. Put this in your mouth."

GROG: "Okay."

[pause]

GROG: "Ouch."

GPS

I LOVE my GPS—the manner in which it ANNOUNCES my driving directions…

Well… it's almost like poetry:

"Two roads diverge in a wood… Please take the road less traveled. Bye."

[recalculating]

“When possible… Please make a U-turn.”

GOOD OLE DAYS

Some days I like to reminisce and think about the “good old days”, back in the days when the years all began with “19”, the days of my youth—back BEFORE the days of smartness phones, the Internet, microwave ovens, GPS technology, mp3 music, streaming video, digital cameras, voice-recognition technology, arthroscopic surgery, angioplasty, laptop computers, and a bunch of other things we now take for granted. I remember those times and think to myself…

Boy. What CRAP times THOSE were.

GREATEST SALES PITCHES OF ALL TIME... 1965 CE: AEROSOL CHEESE

FOODSTUFFS ENGINEER: Now here's a good idea. You know cheese? That foodstuff that comes in big, solid blocks—that we sometimes slice to put on sandwiches? I think we should make it into a liquid, pressurize it, and put it in a Silly String can. That way it would become a CONVENIENCE FOOD. You wouldn't have to unwrap it, slice it, chew it, or digest it. You could just squirt it in one end and out the other.

FOODSTUFFS ENGINEERING MANAGER: Can we actually make cheese DO that?

FOODSTUFFS ENGINEER: Well, of course—it wouldn't actually BE cheese anymore—it would be some sort of yellow, salty, plastic, fairly-tasteless, liquid polymer. But hey, Americans will eat it. Put enough salt, fat and/or sugar in it and we'll eat caulking compound right out of the gun. Besides… it's YELLOW.

FOODSTUFFS ENGINEERING MANAGER: I guess it has potential.

FOODSTUFFS ENGINEER: Sure. In fact, in the future, we could turn it into a whole PRODUCT LINE. We would start out with the Silly String can, but later, redesign the can so it works standing up. That way, you wouldn't even have to tip your head back. Just lean over the can and drink from it like a drinking fountain throughout the day whenever you felt like having a nice, refreshing sip of cheese. In fact, SOMEDAY I envision that we'll be able to forget the can altogether and just run cheese plumbing throughout the house. Then, whenever you felt hungry or thirsty (whatever the feeling is for liquid cheese), you could just turn on the cheese faucet and pour yourself a nice, tall, refreshing glass of cheese.

And if it works well for cheese, how about other foods like liquid beef. In fact, I foresee the day when we will have ALL of our foodstuffs liquefied and delivered to us through our plumbing.

Of course, it wouldn't actually be FOOD any more…

But hey, Americans will eat it.

GULFING

Just to be clear, I hate golf. I don't do it well, I don't know HOW to do it well and, I don't even WANT to know how to do it well.

So, my friends and I went gulfing today. Ya, gulfing. We're pretty bad so it would be inaccurate to call what we do "golfing." "Gulfing" is the more accurate label—especially because of our difficulty with water hazards. Here's why:

With the number of balls we lost, we put more petrochemicals in the water than the Deepwater Horizon.

GO DARK

I guess astrophysicist guys AND astrophysicist lady-womans (making sure to be GENTRY-NEUTRAL here) have looked out into space and done estimates as to how much matter and how much energy there is out there. But when they look at all the space-stuff they CAN see and all the space-stuff they CAN'T see, it turns out that about 102 percent of the matter and energy in our universe is totally UNACCOUNTED for. It's a very mysterious MYSTERY! Think of the ramifications! What does this mean?!!! HERE'S what it means:

It means, there is MORE matter and energy out there… than is ACTUALLY out there! Think of the ramifications! What does THIS mean?!!!

Who knows? Anyway, these same astrophysicist lady-womans AND astrophysicist guys (STILL making sure to be EQUALLY genre-neutral here) tell us that the rest of the unaccounted-for stuff is something called "Dark Energy" and "Dark Mattresses."

Now, the dark energy makes sense to me. I figure it's mostly made up from all the whiny, crappy, venomous, grumbly, critical, complainy stuff I keep hearing on Facebook, Twitter, Myspace, the Food Network (you know who you are, Gordon Ramsey), Altavista and that inflammatory alien Teletubbies show. We've been beaming that crap out into space for years!

I'm not sure about the dark mattresses though. It's a very mysterious MYSTERY!

Gonna have to sleep on it.

GREATEST SALES PITCHES OF ALL TIME... 1969 CE: THE AUTOMOTIVE AIRBAG

AUTOMOTIVE ENGINEER: I have a great idea. What if, when someone crashed their car into something; we inflated a nice comfy pillow in front of them to cushion and comfort their face during the crash?

AUTOMOTIVE ENGINEERING MANAGER: Sounds like a good idea. But things happen pretty fast during a crash. I'm not sure that we could design a pump that could blow the pillow up fast enough.

AUTOMOTIVE ENGINEER: You're absolutely right. I've thought of that and I've got a solution. We'll just stick a shotgun shell in there and fire it off during the crash. That'll pump it up nice and fast.

AUTOMOTIVE ENGINEERING MANAGER: A shotgun shell?

AUTOMOTIVE ENGINEER: We'll remove all the buckshot of course.

AUTOMOTIVE ENGINEERING MANAGER: So, your proposal is, that when people get into a high-speed crash, our car would also shoot them in the face.

AUTOMOTIVE ENGINEER: It would be for their own good.

AUTOMOTIVE ENGINEERING MANAGER: Okay. I'll go see if I can get the necessary development funding.

GIVE ME LIBERTY OR GIVE ME DEBT!

I think I'd make an ABSOLUTELY BRILLIANT political humorist…

Except for the part where you have to KNOW or CARE anything about politics.

CHAPTER EIGHT
Haymakers, Happiness, and Halloween

HUH?

I'm not an actor…

But I play one on TV.

HOT STUFF

It's not the heat...

It's the concussive blast winds and face-melting high-velocity particle field.

HAYMAKER

A HAYMAKER is a wild, violent, knockout punch. So, if your Uncle Pete advises you to MAKE HAY WHILE THE SUN SHINES...

It seems like you might be in for a pretty long and violent day.

HEY! FREE LEMONS!

WHEN LIFE GIVES YOU LEMONS...

Die them blue before gently sanding both ends with 36-grit Carborundum sandpaper. Bake in the oven at 425 degrees for 21-minutes…

Then throw them at someone you hate.

(It'll make you feel better.)

HEY! A TALKING BISON!

I feel like LET THE CHIPS FALL WHERE THEY MAY...

Is probably an old buffalo saying.

HOWS COME?

ME: How come when it's raining cats and dogs, no one EVER calls the ASPCA?

Except me… sometimes.

FRANK: And what's been their response?

ME: They told me to wear a raingoat.

HAPPINESS: $2.35/LB

They say money can't buy happiness—and I believe that's true. But you know what money CAN buy? Gold.

And then I think you can trade THAT for happiness.

(Always thimkin'.)

HOW'S IT HANGIN?

Am I the ONLY one?!!!

I mean, look where they put the towel rack in hotels nowadays! Does anyone ELSE think it's a really, really, REALLY bad idea to hang the towels and washcloths DIRECTLY ABOVE the toilet bowl?

It's getting so I ALMOST don't want to steal them anymore!

HALLOWEEN

Had a fun Halloween this year—innovative I think. Every year up to now, my wife Nancy Matthews and I have passed out candy to the little trick-or-treaters. But with the hazards of sugar (child-obesity, diabetes, tooth decay, etc.) being so frequently spotlighted in the media lately, we decided to search for a better alternative. So, I started thinking, what do kids like? And the answer that I kept coming back to was the same thing that EVERYONE likes: money. But, as we all know, it's tacky to just hand out money. When we're dealing with adults, the solution is to give gift certificates. And I know it's impractical to pass out gift certificates for Halloween, but I liked that basic concept. I needed to find something "spendable" that wasn't money or a gift certificate.

So, we handed out all our returnable bottles and cans to the kids. And the kids—at least the younger ones—seemed genuinely happy. "Hey, Mom! Look! A Budweiser!"

BTW: Does anyone have a good way to clean raw eggs off of… stuff? … You know… pots, pans, dishes… walls, front porches, bushes, car windows…

HEREDITY

The potato doesn't fall far from the tree.

HAPPY THANKSGIVING

Guess how many people burn their houses down each year trying to deep fry a turkey? Go ahead. Guess…

About 4300.

That's right. Over FOUR THOUSAND turkey-brain Iron Chef wannabe Americans somehow manage to barbecue their domiciles each and every year TRYING TO COOK A TURKEY.

And yes, I GET IT. It SOUNDS like a good idea. Because, sure—deep-fried turkey may not be as healthy as roasted, but it TASTES good. Besides, this is your BIG CHANCE TO GET ON THE NEWS! With your mundane, ordinary life; HOW ELSE are you going to do it? I mean Andy Warhol once said, "…everyone will be world-famous for 15 minutes." I say, why not make it your LAST 15 minutes?

(Of course, it looks like you'll have to contend with 4299 others for airtime.)

Here's how simple: Just pour five or six gallons of highly-flammable petroleum into a vat in your kitchen. Then, exercising the most-nominal amount of caution, place a 20-pound tank of ultra-flammable liquid propane down right next to it and light the whole works on fire. Wait for the oil to heat up to around 6000 degrees Fahrenheit and then… toss a big, turkey-shaped block of ice into it. You'll know your turkey's done when the last fireman has left the scene.

Easy. What could go wrong?

(A word of caution: don't be fooled by the simplicity of the process. If not done properly, some of the above steps COULD be risky.) So, I'd like to pass along some safety tips for those of you who are thinking about doing this yourself:

1. Don't.
2. If you must—do it outside—so the neighbors can watch. (Maybe you'll end up on YouTube.)
3. If you must do it in the house, please follow the following

precautions:

a. Line your entire kitchen with asbestos.
b. Seal up all doors and windows to make sure the kitchen is air-tight.
c. Install a Halon 1301 fire suppression system.

By the way, the last three precautions are not for you. They are for the rest of us. When the turkey bomb inevitably goes off, if the smoke and flames don't get you, the Halon is sure to kill you. That way that's one less person like YOU that the rest of us have to contend with running around loose in society.

Me personally? I think I'm going to go cold turkey this year.

Happy Thanksgiving.

HARDSHIP

My wife tried to tell me that there are some places in the world where women have to get up before sunrise every day and walk eight-miles or more through the desert to bring water back for the family. And other places where whole families have to drink their water out of a mud hole. And that there are actually people in America that have to eat DOG FOOD just to stay alive. And she told me to consider the fact that worldwide, about 795 million people are suffering from chronic undernourishment. CHRONIC!

Yes. All very fine stories...

But that's no excuse for BAD SERVICE. HOW DARE YOU serve me TAP WATER with NO LEMON!!! What ARE we? SAVAGES?

???

Now my WHOLE DAY is ruined!!!

HOOMANITY DISASTER

Have you SEEN the news lately? Floods. Shootings. Hurricanes. Mass murders…

NOW my wife tells me, MORE Kardashians are on the way! Apparently, three of the high-handed haughties are PREGNANT!

For once…

WHY can't humanity at least CATCH A BREAK?!!

HOOMAN HAIRBALLS

Did you ever have all the little hairs under your armpit roll together into a little ball all by themselves, spontaneously—just from your arm action—such that they formed into a little knot, such that when you suddenly raised your arm above your head, it pulled all those little hairs and made your eyes water, such that when you raised your arm in class to ask a question, and your eyes began to water, the teacher thought that it was going to be a really pithy, poignant, and soulful question; but it was really only a question about Robert Fulton's cotton gin and whether or not it was JUST an alcoholic drink, or an alcoholic drink AND a card game?

Or is it just me?

HALF A GLASS

The pessimist sees the glass as half empty. The optimist sees the glass as half full.

The pragmatist smiles and puts his goldfish in it.

HEALTHCOST CARES

In recent decades, we here in America have all been wrestling with the rising costs of health care. I believe that I can show by example that there are two basic reasons for this.

It costs me $750 to go to the doctor today. When I was little, my parents would take me to the family doctor. When it came time to "settle up", he would charge them $18 and a couple packs of cigarettes for that same visit and we would be "square." Today I go to the pharmacist and they charge me $75 to get a prescription filled. When I was little, my parents could get that same prescription filled for 35 cents AND they could test their TV and radio tubes for FREE while they waited.

So here is my premise: I believe that rising health care costs are due to two primary factors: 1) doctors are charging us more money and 2) druggists are charging us more money.

Conversely, in Canada, the Canadian doctor would charge nothing for that same visit and the Canadian pharmacist would charge nothing for that same prescription. Now, we all know that some of this part of this difference in cost differential is due to the exchange rate—but I think if we just try to fix that, we are simply not thinking BIG enough. We need to go after the REAL problem. It all comes down to this:

If the Canadians were able to get their health care costs down to zero, I think we Americans should be able to do TWICE as good.

(Yes, sometimes it feels like I'm the only one THIMKING here.)

HAWAIIAN PIZZA?

Pineapple on pizza? Not a fan. As Chef Emeril Lagasse might have said

(AND, it's never been proven that he HASN'T said this), "No good ever came from sprinkling fruit on a pizza—BAM!!!"

However, my feeling is, if you're one of those poor lost souls who is COMPELLED to put pineapple on a pizza, then I say why stop there? You might as well go "all the way" and sprinkle some shredded coconut on top, splash a bunch of rum in the tomato sauce, and stab a little paper umbrella in the middle.

Pizza Colada.

(Go big or stay home, I always say—BAM!!!)

HEIL HERR HEIR

What if Hitler had had a son? And what if the son had been named after the father—Adolf Messershmidt Hitler Jr. or something like that? Everyone would have called him Adolf Jr. or Fuher Jr. or some kind of "Junior" name because, after all, he would have been the despot's son. And to my ear, that would have sounded like a German fast food franchise item:

"I'll have a Furher Jr. with extra mayo… And a panzer shake… Oh! And some French fries; because of course, we now OWN France."

HI, STANDURDS

On some days I have these "bursts" of what I guess you would call "brilliance", "inspiration" or "creative genius." And on these days, I am able to produce things that are PROFOUNDLY and SOLIDLY mediocre.

But I can't maintain that level of performance EVERY day.

What am I?

A machine??

HORSE CONFUSION

We do NOT have Pegasus, the splendid FLYING HORSE in our real world. It is but a mythical WINGED STEED that is sadly, only the stuff of legends and lore.

We DO, however, have the HORSEFLY which is an irritating, biting, FLYING BUG that DOES exist in our real world—and in great numbers.

[sigh]

So close.

HEAD BUTT

If the President of the United States chose not to wear any underwear…

Would that make him Commando in Chief?

HMM…

I wonder what penguins wear on casual Friday.

HOW DUMB WERE THEY?

I think when someone says someone else is "as dumb as a bag of hammers", they should have to specify whether or not they meant CLAW HAMMERS or BALL-PEEN hammers.

Otherwise, how are WE going to know just exactly how dumb that person was?

HOT SUMMER NIGHTS

I read that crickets make that chirpy sound by rubbing their wings together, all fast and vibratey-like. I also read that you can tell the temperature outside by listening to how fast the crickets chirp—the hotter the temperature, the more chirps per minute.

And you think YOU get chaffed armpits on a hot night! BAHAHAHAHAHA!!!

[crickets chirping]

HOW TO DRIVE ON THE WRONG SIDE OF THE ROAD

AUTHOR'S NOTE: THE FOLLOWING ESSAY CONTAINS PASSAGES THAT MAY POSSIBLY OFFER ACTUAL, VALID, REAL-WORLD USEFUL AND/OR HELPFUL INFORMATION. (My apologies.)

In the late 1700s, a few young colonial pranksters decided to play a little gag on their English BFFs by dressing up as "Native Colonials" (as they were politically-correctly referred to back in those days) and tossing some of their buds' favorite tasty hot beverages into Boston Harbor. Not to be outdone, the British lads decided to punk their American mates by driving their horses and wagons on the wrong side of the road–kind of like a game of Colonial Chicken. For safety sake, the English boys wore bright, high-visibility red coats to avoid head-on collisions with the American blokes which is where we get our common nickname for the British: "limeys."

Shortly afterward, the British found that building a vast, worldwide empire was a good way to meet chicks. So off they went offering exclusive British Empire memberships to a multitude of needy, less fortunate countries.

Fast-forward a couple hundred plus years, and we find that nearly everywhere in the world where the British had historically offered to manage other people's countries for them, the left-handed driving game of Colonial Chicken has curiously caught on as the preferred motoring mode.

My wife and I are currently vacationing in the Cayman Islands (a British colony) where I've had to learn to drive on the left side of the road as a matter of survival—when in Rome, do as the Romanians do, I always say.

To some, driving on the left may sound like a daunting task. To others, it may sound like a "no-brainer." The fact is, it's somewhere in between. Should you find yourself in a similar situation, I have developed Four Rules for Driving on the Wrong Side of the Road which have thus far preserved my and my wife's lives:

1. Drive on the Left.
Duh. Isn't that the point? Yes, it is. It is EXACTLY the point. But, driving on the left doesn't come automatically to us "Colonials." So, the point is to MAKE IT CONSCIOUS–all the time. And I do that by repeating rule number one to myself when I do practically anything–when I get into the car, when I make a turn, when I pull out into traffic, when I dry my socks in the microwave—practically ANYTHING.

I find this rule especially helpful when driving in areas without lane markers like parking lots, residential streets... people's front lawns.

Drive on the Left. REPETITION IS KEY.

2. Look to the Right

Because traffic in the closest lane always comes at us from the left, looking left has been ingrained into us Americans. As you might suspect, it's just the opposite for those pesky countries that drive on the left. "Always look right." I got this tip from the American guy working the rental car counter and it's a great one.

Again, repetition is key. I say this to myself whenever I pull out into traffic, enter a roundabout or otherwise merge with traffic. And this rule is an absolute MUST for American pedestrians. ALWAYS LOOK TO THE RIGHT before crossing the street. Curb traffic comes from the wrong direction and nothing says "ruined vacation" faster than an unscheduled, impromptu trip to the ER/morgue.

3. Right Turns are Hard

Okay, they're not THAT hard. They're like North American left turns. But the point is, not only do you have to cut across a lane of oncoming traffic, but you ALSO have to remember to cross over into the LEFT-HAND lane as you finish the turn. So, I always use rule one together with rule three. When making a right-hand turn, I remind myself that Right Turns are Hard so I'll be extra diligent in looking for oncoming traffic. Then I remind myself to Drive on the Left so as to avoid the dreaded Colonial-Chicken-game-effect.

Bonus tip: After completing any right turn, check for wreckage in the rear-view mirror.

4. Left Turns are Easy

Tell me you didn't see THAT coming. Yep, just like right turns at home (MY home)—only backward. Again, this is a rule I always use in combination with another rule. I use rule four and rule two together infallibly. I remind myself that Left Turns are Easy which cues me to turn into the nearest (left) lane without crossing oncoming traffic. But before I turn, I remind myself to Look to the Right because that's where the traffic I'm merging with will be coming from.

Although I don't have to consciously remind myself to Drive on the Left because the Left Turns are Easy rule automatically directs me into the correct lane, I generally do so anyway... because I'm insecure.

So, there they are—my Four Rules for Driving on the Wrong Side of the Road. I know that they're not rocket surgery—they're not MEANT to be. They are meant to KEEP ME ALIVE. They are things that I need to keep in my conscious mind if I want to avoid an embarrassing fatal traffic accident.

The point is: they work for me. They are a way of organizing my wrong-way driving knowledge so that it's available to me at all times. When I keep repeating these rules to myself, I find that they're there, on "the tip of my brain" when I need to make quick driving decisions.

So, this is the part where I ought to make a fancy, highfalutin, legal-sounding DISCLAIMER. Only I'm not a lawyer so it might be a tad lowfalutin:

I'm not a driving expert. I'm not a driving professional. I'm not even wearing SHOES. I'm just an old man with a computer, a wife and a Facebook who has managed to stay alive while driving a rental car around a tropical island for a few weeks or so. I'm NOT MANDATING, I'm NOT RECOMMENDING—I'm NOT EVEN SUGGESTING; I'm just SHARING the things that work for me. If I WAS recommending, I'd say: Use these rules at your own risk. If you turn your rental car into a popular new dive site just offshore of some Caribbean paradise because you were trying out my rules... Oops. YOUR BAD. See you on the news.

Also, some of the historical information might not be completely accurate.

CHAPTER NINE
Inspiration, Irony, and Ideas

I'M AT CGM'S DOJO...

I'm at Chief Grand Master's dojo right now with my daughter, Kristen Matthews. My back hurts. My legs hurt. And Chief Grand Master had us kicking each other ALL MORNING LONG. I'm sore. I'm miserable. I'm in pain.

This is the BEST!

I'M SOMEBODY

[Fade in]

I put my name into IMDB yesterday, just for gits and shiggles. As it turns out, I'm actually SOMEBODY. There was a character (and this part is ABSOLUTELY true) named "Bob Matthews" in the 1956 box-office smash hit movie SWAMP WOMEN. Really.

Although I've never actually seen (or even heard of) this movie, I'm going to give you a quick synopsis based on the half-paragraph provided by IMDB:

It's a (possibly gripping) story (or not) of three (possibly highly attractive) women (or not) who execute a (possibly daring) prison escape in order to go recover their stash of (most likely) stolen diamonds which they hid... wait for it... IN A SWAMP! It stars Marie Windsor, Carole Matthews (what are the odds?) and Beverly Garland as (I'm guessing) the three swamp women?

IMDB has conveniently included some of (the possibly handsome and charming) Bob Matthews riveting dialog on their website. Before I present this masterful example of cinematographic dialogery, let me set the scene for you:

In this scene, Bob is trying to "seduce" Billie when... [spoiler alert: skip to the end if you don't want to read that "he is rudely interrupted by Vera"] ... he is rudely interrupted by Vera.

Below is the ACTUAL DIALOG, cut and pasted from IMDB—ABSOLUTELY unaltered by me (because it would be SO hard to improve upon):

BOB MATTHEWS: What can I do for you?
BILLIE: Anything you like.
BOB MATTHEWS: What if I don't like?
BILLIE: You will.
VERA: You dirty little dumb broad!

Unfortunately, that small sample was all that there was. Probably the rest of it just wasn't as good.

[Fade to black]

Sit Ubu. Sit...

Good dog.

INSPIRATION FROM THE COUNT OF MONTY CRISCO

EDMOND DANTES: Life is a storm, my young friend. You will bask in the sunlight one moment, be shattered on the rocks the next. What makes you a man is what you do when that storm comes. You must look into that storm and shout as you did in Rome. Do your worst, for I will do mine!

ME: Then never let it be said, Eddie, that I did not do my wurst!

("Always leave 'em with a good sausage joke," my father used to say.)

I HEAR DEAD PEOPLE

If you ever go to a funeral home, and the body suddenly sits bolt upright in the coffin and starts yapping at you…

Pay it no mind.

It's only the embalming juice talking.

IDEAS

You might ask how I consistently come up with so many unique ideas for daily Facebook posts. I might answer, that if you search with the RIGHT ATTITUDE and with an OPEN MIND; you can find inspiration and ideas nearly ANYWHERE.

To prove that point, today I looked under my armpit…

Nothing…

Well… THIS post… So…

Nothing.

IF…

IF I HAD A NICKEL for every time someone gave me a dollar…

Because hey! You know…

Free nickels!

I LOVE THE CLOUD

I love THE CLOUD. I keep all sorts of things in THE CLOUD. It's great for keeping my information organized and readily available. And it's so versatile. Once I store things up there, I can use my computer, smartness phone, or various other devices to conveniently retrieve it. It seems like we've come SO FAR in such a SHORT TIME—technologically speaking.

It probably wasn't more than a dozen generations ago, if you wanted to get something down out of a cloud, you had to ride your horse over to Crazy Old Ben Franklin's place and get him to fish it down for you with a kite.

IDEA MACHINE

I get some of my best and most creative writing ideas while doing mindless tasks like showering, washing the car or working out. I just got out of a 15-minute shower and here's what I came up with:

"Zounds, Tammy! We'll burn your bridges behind you when we get to it!" [cue laugh track].

While I rather like the employment of the underutilized exclamation "ZOUNDS" (gives it sort of a Dudley Doright-ish feel), I feel that the concept—the full Gestalt—lacks sophistication, finesse and/or depth. I think it needs more development. Which means I need more creative ideas. So maybe I'll go for a run.

Oh, wait...

I don't run.

IRONING BORED

My wife, Nancy and I attended an out-of-town wedding yesterday. In preparation for the event, I discovered that—depending upon your standards—I MAY or may NOT know how to iron a shirt.

If you count poking at a wrinkly, defenseless garment with a dangerous, hot, steamy, household appliance for upwards of half-an-hour; then I DO know how to iron.

If, in your opinion, there should be an obvious and discernible IMPROVEMENT in how the garment looks after I'm done "ironing", then I might not actually know what I'm doing.

(Ya… So probably the second one.)

IT'S A WONDERFUL HEIST

I believe that every time someone robs a liquor store…

An angel gets his wings.

(Or is it a "robber gets his spirits"?)

I-275 OBSTRUCTIONS

I don't know if anyone else saw it, but there was a sofa in the middle of southbound I-275 yesterday afternoon. It was just sitting there a little north of Canton—obstructing traffic in the middle lane. It was in pretty good condition. It was upright and resting on all four legs. All the couch cushions were neatly in place. It was well-centered in its lane and facing directly southbound.

In my opinion, it actually looked pretty good sitting there. There was only one slight problem.

With all that heavy rush hour traffic honking, skidding and swerving around…

It was a lot harder getting that thing set up than I had originally imagined.

(I'm going back today to add a floor lamp and a coffee table… maybe set out a few coasters.)

IGNORANCE OF YOUTH

Remember back when you were a kid and you thought grownups were actually grown up?

And then YOU "grew up"?

IRONY

I think the wife fails to see the irony in the fact that she has told me REPEATEDLY, OVER and OVER, 20-30 times—

That her MOTHER is starting to suffer short-term memory loss.

INPORTANT QWESTIONS

I'm sure this goes without saying, but not everyone thinks like me.

For instance, have you ever wondered what the OPPOSITE of "peas and carrots" would be? Would it be "carrots and peas"? Or, would it be "cars and pearots"? Or… would it be the other way around?

See what I mean? If it were not for people like me, these kinds of questions would be left… not only unANSWERED… but unASKED.

Yes, sometimes it feels like I'm the only one THIMKING around here.

IS THAT TRUE?

THE TRUTH WILL SET YOU FREE!*

*I think maybe that doesn't apply to confessions.

I JUST KNOW!

I just KNOW that I'm going to be on this earth for many more years to come…

Because I've just got SO many more people to torment.

(Good Morning Nancy Matthews.)

INFORMATION UNDERLOAD

My smartness phone woke me during a heavy rainstorm (true story), at 5:30 in the morning, with THIS urgent and informative message:

"Rain will continue."

As it was still raining eight-seconds later when I fell back to sleep, I can assure everyone that it WAS accurate. But I'm unsure of the purpose of this unwelcome, mid-slumber morsel of indisputable-yet-pointless "information." Was I to build an ark? Were "they" just checking in with me to see if it was okay to continue the rain? Or perhaps Captain Obvious has hijacked my cell phone provider for his own public service announcement purposes. I can't wait for tomorrow's early morning smartness communique:

"Earth rotation will CONTINUE…

"Until further notice."

("Is that okay with you, Bob?")

I DON'T MIND

A mind is a terrible thing to waist.

I COULD BE A CINEMATOLOGIST!

I think Hollywood should make a movie about a young girl who is kidnapped by bad guys. However, (and here's the good part) her father is a badass kind of a guy with "a very particular set of skills." Skills that he has acquired over a very long career. Skills that would make him a nightmare for people like the ones that kidnapped his daughter. Skills that would allow him to spend the rest of the movie traveling the world, tracking down his daughter, and randomly killing hundreds of ethnic-looking bad guys—but with complete and total political correctness.

But I wouldn't make the skillful, badass kind of a guy some heretofore UNKNOWN character that we had NEVER HEARD OF before this movie. I'd make the father-character part of some well-known successful movie franchise. In short, I would make the kidnapping victim the daughter of JAMES BOND. That's right. James Bond. And I would call the movie:

Taken: Not Stirred.

(Okay. I think my job is done here.)

INFERNAL CONFLICT

If I am not with me, then I am against me.

—NORMAN BATES

CHAPTER TEN
June, Justice, and Japan

JUNE 27, 2017: THE END OF COMMON DECENCY

What follows is technically "the beginning." My VERY FIRST Facebook post.

I published it on June 27, 2017, at the age of 64. That's right. I waited until I was 64 until I STARTED using Facebook. Before this, I just "wasn't interested."

Then both of our kids "grew up" and moved out of our house, and Facebook became a way to "stay in touch." (Ironically, MY Facebook has become a way to "stay OUT of touch" [with reality]). So, who KNEW things would turn out this way?!! This ENTIRE BOOK grew from the following simple and humble (translation: "crappy") post. In a way, I feel like it's kind of THE NATURAL ORDER OF THINGS.

Like fungus.

The post says it all: "I'm not proud." I guess I'm really just including it for the sake of some sort of "historical completeness." Kind of an OCD thing. But I AM proud that I had the courage to START and to CONTINUE. So, what follows can be taken as a LIFE-LESSON for all of us. And that lesson would be… Don't EVER write crap like this:

> Helloooo… thump, thump, thump. Is this thing on? …
>
> I've finally decided to enter the 20th century—technologically speaking. (I hear they have talking movies now). Imonna get on Facebook.

Ya, I know. Everyone else (including my kids) have been on it for decades. Not me. I've been fashionably behind-the-times.

So, this is my first post. I'm not proud. I'm just sayin...

Nap time.

JAPANESE BAKERY

If I ever open a Japanese bakery, I think I'll call it...

Wait for it...

THE LAND OF THE RISING BUN.

TAH-DAH!!!

JUNKER

My brain hasn't been running very well lately. It's been running kind of rough and it stalls out once in a while. And it's also been kind of hard to start—especially on cold mornings. I tried dumping a little alcohol in it to try and get it going—but that didn't seem to help AT ALL.

I had my doctor take a look at it and she said it might be the camshaft. One of the lobes—possibly one of the frontal lobes—is a little off-kilter. Anyway, she said it's going to have to be REPLACED and THAT would cost about $3,500.

So, as you might imagine, I can't afford that right now. So, I'm just going to have to limp along with my brain "as-is" and try and keep it going until I can afford a new one.

Now if I can just get this annoying EXHAUST problem taken care of.

JUST JUSTICE

I believe in justice—reasonable, appropriate, rightful justice—justice that demands that the punishment befits the crime—no matter how harsh that punishment may need to be.

For instance, in the case of identity theft:

I believe that in terms of a reasonable, appropriate, rightful punishment; if someone steals my identity…

They should be forced to keep it.

CHAPTER ELEVEN
King Solomon, Kitchens, and Kidhood

KITCHEN MEMORIES

When I was a little boy, my mom used to make homemade meatloaf...

And I got to lick the spoon!

KING SOLOMON'S WIVES

Guess how many wives King Solomon had. Go ahead guess.

According to the Bible (on which I am NOT an expert on AND the Ultimate Book of Useless Information [of which I AM somewhat of an aficionado]): 700! 700 WIVES! Think of the TOILET PAPER. If you think the Amazon rainforest is in jeopardy NOW!

And it gets worse:

He was also seeing 300 women ON THE SIDE. Ya. 300 mistresses (they called them concubines in those days).

Where did he get the time... or the energy? That's a total of a THOUSAND WOMEN! A THOUSAND!

I mean JUST THE LYING ALONE would have almost certainly occupied most of his time:

(to 304th wife) "No Dear. Those baggy silk pants don't make you look fat."
(to 305th wife) "No Dear. Those baggy silk pants don't make you look

fat."
(to 306th wife) "No Dear. Those baggy silk pants don't make you look fat."
(to 307th wife) "No Dear. Those baggy silk pants don't make you"...

KIDHOOD MEMORIES

When I was kid I had a friend named RUSTY. I miss those days.

Also, I think it's kinda sad that no one names their kids after any of the metal oxides anymore.

KIM JONG ILLinois

Apparently, North Korea now has atomic weapons chomping at the nuclear bit to take out Chicago's Shedd Aquarium at a moment's notice—SIMULTANEOUSLY THREATENING THE NATION'S CHICAGO DEEP-DISH PIZZA SUPPLY. In the spirit of that old saying: BETTER SAFE THAN THE DEVIL YOU DON'T KNOW, I firmly believe we should be training our children to hide under their desks again.

I think "nuclear death avoidance via the skilled employment of-academic furniture" is a collective skill that we, as a nation, are rapidly losing. As time passes there are perilously fewer and fewer of us patriotic, boomer-type citizens officially trained in the art of "ducking and covering."

Besides, I think if we're not going to pay our teachers properly, we should at least give them something entertaining to watch.

KEEP THE CHANGE

Years ago, my wife and I were sitting at our computer, doing our taxes, when I started getting odd chest pains. At the hospital, they determined that I was suffering a mild heart attack (true story). So, they performed angioplasty and installed a stent. And, after it was all over, my doctor told me I was going to have to make some drastic lifestyle changes.

So, I got an accountant.

CHAPTER TWELVE
Legs, Light, and Lemons

LUMPY LEGS

For the past few years, I have been suffering from a condition commonly known as "lumpy legs." And when I say "commonly known as" what I mean is, that's how I commonly know it.

Anyway. I went to the doctor and the doctor said, "No more monkeys jumping on the bed!" So, I stopped going to THAT doctor and I went to a chiropractor. He, in turn, referred me to a therapeutical massage therapist.

And when I first visited my therapeutical massage therapist, she told me my leg muscles were like concrete—to the point where she was just going to paint lane markers on them and refund my money. She told me that muscles aren't supposed to CRUNCH. She told me my legs were the WORST she'd ever seen in her entire career. This, of course, made me proud.

Finally, I'm GOOD at something. I mean, I'm at the TOP of the list. Sure, it may be the list of the ABSOLUTE WORST… but… I'M AT THE TOP! To me, it's like finishing last in a marathon. It's a source of notoriety even though some might possibly look at it as a source of shame. It's good and bad—but mostly GOOD. You may have furnished DEAD LAST. But, on the bright side, you didn't DIE finishing dead last. You might have been the worst at THE RUNNING, but you were the BEST at THE NOT DYING. And I think there ought to be a TROPHY for that!

Anyway, I think I've been somewhat of A CHALLENGE for her (the massaganist). She's been crumpling, crunching, mashing, bruising, squishing, and pulverizing my legs for a couple years now with limited success. But she keeps AT it! I gotta give her THAT. (I also gotta give her money.)

I asked her if she felt threatened by those massage soap bars you get in hotels with the bumps on them. She asked ME if I felt threatened by the fact that I was lying face-down, with my back to her, vulnerable and defenseless with my face resting on a tiny, padded toilet seat.

She thinks my problem is SYSTEMIC. She thinks my problem is CHEMICAL. She thinks I got lumpy legs from taking STATINS for more than a decade.

Statins work by interfering with your body's production of cholesterol. Side effects may include liver damage, muscle damage, elevated blood sugar, pyromania, dismemberment, demonic possession, loss of urine, and advanced Forrest Gump Disease. My cardiologist said these statins are meant to keep me from dying. But secretly, deep inside—

I think, at best they will only keep me from dying COMFORTABLY.

LEMONS (AGAIN)

When life gives you lemons…

Politely decline them and go buy ice cream.

LIFE TIME FATNESS

I'm at "the gym", LIFE TIME FATNESS, trying to remove about six decades of body putty in about 45 minutes.

So far, I'm not impressed with the results.

Maybe there's a pill I can take.

LIMITING BELIEFS

I believe that much of our success in life is dependent upon our ATTITUDE. For instance, if you truly believe in your heart that THE SKY IS THE LIMIT and ACT as if this was ABSOLUTELY TRUE…

I think you just might have a hard time getting a job at NASA.

LEGAL TENDON

Do you remember when you were a little kid and you saved a little bit of your 25-cent allowance every week until you had a GIANT amount of money—MORE than a dollar? So, you bugged your mom to take you to Edgewater amusement park for a day, but she said you couldn't afford to go to Edgewater because it would cost an "arm and a leg" to get in and you didn't have enough money. So instead she said she'd take you to Atlantic Mills department store to buy something really good, but what she really meant was she'd make your FATHER take you to Atlantic Mills department store to buy something really good because back in those days, moms didn't DRIVE.

So, after some arm-twisting and ear-pulling, your dad drove you to Atlantic Mills department store to buy something really good. And when you guys FINALLY got inside the store, he turned you loose in the toy section to shop all by yourself, vulnerable and unsupervised, while he went to look at screwdrivers—because that's what good parents DID back in those days.

After HOURS of looking through the toys, you finally found what you wanted and showed it to your dad. He asked you if you REALLY wanted it because it was going to cost you an "arm and a leg" and you said, "Yes. You did."

So, he took you up to the checkout counter and you handed your money to the cashier. And when they rang it up, you found out it only cost an arm. So, you could either get back a leg in change or have the cashier give you store credit. So, you asked your dad what you should do.

And he told you, "Take the store credit. That way, next time you come in...

"You'll already be a leg up."

LIGHT IS REALLY FAST!

Light is REALLY fast!

Light travels at 186,000 miles per hour. One HUNDRED and eighty-six THOUSAND! Do you know how fast that is?!!

Flick on a light switch. BOOM!!! One second later—those photons are one hundred and eighty-six THOUSAND miles away!

Can you REALLY comprehend just how incomprehensibly fast that REALLY is? Of course, you can't! It's almost unknowable to REALLY be able to know this. Our feeble human minds are too tiny, too limited, too inadequate to comprehend the incomprehensible scales of our mysterious, enigmatic universe. That's where I come in...

Due to my extensive scientific and engineering training and experience, I habitually and routinely deal with such extreme velocities, distances, and related phenomena. Listen carefully, and this will all make sense to you in a moment.

Trust me. I'm an engineer.

As I stated earlier, light travels at 186,000 miles per hour. There are exactly eight furlongs in a statute mile which means that light travels at

1,488,000 furlongs per hour. There are exactly 168 hours in a standard U.S. week. This tells us that light moves at the blinding speed of 249,984,000 furlongs per standard U.S. week. A single fortnight is made up of exactly two standard U.S. weeks. All these things taken together reveal to us that light travels at the hyper-brisk, bat-out-of-hell rate of 499,968,000 furlongs per fortnight.

499,968,000! Four hundred and ninety-nine MILLION, nine hundred and sixty-eight THOUSAND—which I hope to God you realize is a REALLY big number—almost half a BILLION! This clearly, incontrovertibly, and UNDENIABLY demonstrates to us… that light is REALLY fast.

I hope this helps.

LOST

ON APRIL 27, 1882, THE LITERARY WORLD LOST A GREAT WRITER AND POET:

Ralph Where's-Waldo Emerson…

[pause]

Oh, WAIT!

I found him.

LOSING INCHES

I got myself a new cardiologist about a year ago. He bills himself as "The Plant Doctor" because his philosophy is to control health and chronic disease with lifestyle choices as much as possible and to minimize the use of medications. And, of course, this includes eating a lot of plants. So, he's had me on a totally plant-based diet and, in terms of my health, I've made good progress. But eventually, I plateaued.

He told me he wants to see me lose a few pounds and improve my health metrics even more. In short, I need to "do better." He told me, "If you want to LOSE THE INCHES, you have to get into the gym."

So, I did. And after several months, I decided to measure myself and it turns out he was RIGHT.

I think I'm about four inches shorter.

LIFE IS HECTIC!!!

Lately, I've been running around like a chicken with its legs cut off!!!

LEMMINGADE?

When life gives you lemmings...

Make parachutes.

CHAPTER THIRTEEN
Morpheus, Michigan, and Motorcycles

MARKETING 1.01

I feel like SHIZNIT would be a GREAT name for a candy bar:

Rich dark chocolate, crunchy peanuts, smooth plastic nougat—

SHIZNIT…

IT'S the shiznit!

MOCKASINS

Don't judge a man until you have walked a mile in his car.

MY LAMENT

I know this sounds REALLY weird, but it's actually the truth. I really HAVE had this actual thought during some of my private quieter moments:

I sometimes lament about the trees that have given their lives…

Just so I can wipe my butt.

MY DREAM

IT'S ALWAYS BEEN MY DREAM to be able to yodel...

Wait...

NO IT HASN'T!

MOTORCYCLE GUY

Stopping for a red light, I pulled up behind a guy on a motorcycle. Written across the back of his T-shirt (and I'm not making this part up) were the following wistful words:

Huntin bucks
and drivin trucks
That's how I roll.

And I thought to myself: The haiku just isn't what it used to be.

MY FIRST HAIKU

You know I've had some "credibility issues" in the past. And when I say "I've had some 'credibility issues' in the past," I mean I've had some "credibility issues" for the last six-plus decades (so far). But that's not the point...

The point is, that I realize that even though it sounds "made up", I REALLY DID see some stranger on a motorcycle wearing a Huntin bucks T-shirt. And this event has inspired me to write my very own haiku. Here it is. This is it. Hope you like it.

MY FIRST HAIKU by Bob Matthews

I am weary, Claire.
Fallen down and can't get up.
Maimed my uvula.

Wow. This haiku stuff is EASY. Who knew?

Probably Claire. But she couldn't tell me because…

Her uvula.

MAN'S BEST FIEND

They say a dog is man's best friend. I have my doubts.

So far, it's been almost a month and King Cosmo STILL hasn't accepted my friend request.

MY PROBLEM… DEFINITELY, MY PROBLEM

Here is an actual conversation (not making this up) that took place between my dad and me—NOT when I was seven, NOT when I was 17, or even 27—but when I was in my late 50's:

MY DAD: You know what your problem is?

57-YEAR-OLD ME: No. What?

MY DAD: Your problem is you make all your own decisions.

57-YEAR-OLD ME: Ya. Shoulda DECIDED to ignore that question.

MILFORD MEMORIES

We just got back from a street fair, ironically named MILFORD MEMORIES.

I say that because I saw so many there that were WASTED. And tomorrow…

They will have NO memories of Milford.

MAJOR LEAGUE INNOVATION

I went to a Detroit Tigers major league baseball game yesterday. I'm not bragging. I'm not saying I'm proud. I'm just stating the facts.

Now, those of you that know me personally (and some of those who know me impersonally), know that if I'm anything—I'm a THINKER. Most of the others there, were just watching the game. But not me. Sure, I was watching. But I was also THINKING—thinking, and observing, and… thinking. And here's what I think I noticed:

Most of the field looks REALLY NICE—like a REALLY NICE lawn. It's all grassy and cut in a checkerboardy, stripey kind of way—not in an ostentatious checkerboardy, stripey kind of way—but in a REALLY NICE checkerboardy, stripey kind of way. And, when the sun hits it at just the right angle… it looks green.

But then, there's this one part of the field—the part where they keep all the bases and plastic plates. It's just dirt. DIRT. They call it THE INFIELD (I guess because it's "in" the "field").

At one point in the game, the Comerica Park head infield guy—I don't know what they call him—the INFIELD ADMIRAL maybe. Anyway, at one point in the game, the infield admiral decides that the infield is starting to look too lumpy. So, he gets a bunch of guys together, six or eight maybe and they go and look around in the back room. And they drag out EVERYTHING they can find. Old garden tools, big hunks of old chain link fence, sticks, great big garden rakes, stuff like that.

Then the infield admiral STOPS THE GAME. And these guys drag all this old junk across the infield and knock down all the lumps, cover over all the little divots and smooth out the whole infield dirt pile. And (credit where credit's due) they do a REALLY NICE job. They're all careful to wear the same clothes to work so they all look alike, which is a REALLY NICE effect. And they walk in REALLY NICE, tidy formations as if they'd all been in marching band—or the army (although not necessarily OUR army). And I gotta say, when they're done, everything looks REALLY NICE.

But here's what I'm thinking. There's six or eight guys involved. And during EACH AND EVERY Detroit Tigers major league baseball game, they have to go dig up all this stuff, drag it onto the field, and then pull it around like a coordinated squad of farming combines threshing their way through amber waves of grain. I'm thinking, it just seems like there's a LOT going on. It seems very INEFFICIENT. And don't get me wrong. I think when they're done it looks REALLY NICE. But...

I think there's a LOT of money to be made for the person that invents the INFIELD ZAMBONI.

Once we get the infield Zamboni thing going, I think another great tradition would be; after every time the Tigers scored a run, fans would throw Tigerfish out onto the infield.

You're welcome.

MORPHEUS SIGHS

MORPHEUS: Like everyone else, you were born into bondage, born into a prison that you cannot smell, or taste, or touch. A prison for your mind.

Unfortunately, no one can be told what the Matrix is. You have to see it for yourself. This is your last chance. After this, there is no turning back. You take the blue pill—the story ends, you wake up in your bed and you believe whatever you want to. You take the red pill—you stay in Wonderland and I show you how deep the rabbit hole goes.

[Morpheus has both his hands open, holding one pill in each.]

ME: Do you have any Advil? ... Advil? No? How about an Aleve? … No?

[Morpheus sighs]

MUSING

Most days I feel like I'm channeling my inner Cuckoo's Nest.

MY HAIKU TUESDAY

I'm thinking of starting a "regular" thing called "Haiku Tuesday." What I mean by "Haiku Tuesday" is that I am going to write a Haiku and publish it today (which is Tuesday). What I mean by "regular" is (looking backward) last week Haiku Tuesday was ACTUALLY on a Saturday—but I didn't call it that. And (looking forward) I probably won't EVER do it again.

So, here it is—Tuesday's (today's) "regular" haiku:

Haiku-schmaiku, Earl.
These haiku rules are too hard.
Dumb Haiku.

MR. SPOCK

I've often wondered about that Mr. Spock guy from Star Trek.

When he was just a tiny little alien Vulcan pup, why they didn't just go ahead and crop his ears at the same time they docked his tail?

MY THOUGHTS

I think that the words that you think that you thought that you heard me say, are NOT the words that I think that I thought that I had intended to say. But the words that I think that I thought that you thought that you heard me say, ARE really the words that I think that I thought that you thought you understood.

I think.

MONDAY, JANUARY 1, 2018: SOME PHILOSOPHICAL THOUGHTS FROM BOB'S WORLD

Here it is: January first of 2018—the first day of a new year and I've just gone to the bathroom.

And as I was sitting there in the bathroom, I realized that the stuff I had just eliminated was from LAST year—probably things I had eaten YESTERDAY. And it came to me that this was an excellent metaphor for life. I was leaving behind the stuff of yesteryear. I was literally letting go of the past—flushing away the waste, the dreck, the biological wreckage from last year—from my PAST.

And now, I would go and eat breakfast—to begin to nourish myself in the NEW year—to begin to REBUILD my body, my soul, and maybe some pancreatic tissue. And it was as if, by eating 2018 food, I was embracing the future.

But then I realized that I had ACQUIRED the food that I was going to eat LAST YEAR, so I was in actuality, STILL EMBRACING THE PAST. And even if I went out and bought fresh, new food today on the first day of the year—it undoubtedly was ALMOST CERTAINLY produced LAST year. So, I was purging my body of 2017 debris but replenishing it with YESTERDAY'S nutrients—which was NOT the excellent metaphor for life that I was trying to embody.

And then I found it—in a dark, dusty corner of our kitchen pantry—a lone can of dark red kidney beans from 2015. And it suddenly occurred to me that by eating these beans, I would be eating the stuff of 2015.

Yes! I would be TIME TRAVELING (which everyone knows is a very advanced, FUTURISTIC concept). So, it was as if by eating this can of magical beans, I was invoking the notion of time-travel and thus, embracing the future!

And isn't that what life is all about?

Happy New Year to ALL of my most excellent friends. And here's some EXCELLENT advice from "the future":

Don't eat old food.

(Feeling a little queasy.)

MY REFLECTIONS ON MIRRORS

I've been thinking about this for a long time:

I think that when we look into a mirror, that the person on the other side (who looks exactly like a backward us) is actually the REAL person—and that WE are actually just THEIR REFLECTION. Here's why:

When I'm on my side of the mirror with my dog (King Cosmo), and he happens to glance into the mirror at the backward us, he's never even the SLIGHTEST bit interested. He doesn't seem to care at all. He doesn't bark, stare, sniff, examine or ponder what he sees in the mirror. He just ignores it—just as if it WASN'T EVEN THERE. Just like it was simply any old random part of the wall.

And isn't that exactly what you'd expect a dog REFLECTION to do?

MY BUCKET LIST

What's on YOUR bucket list?

I think someday, I'd like to give a TED Talk…

Bahahahahahahahahahahaha!
BaHaHaHaHaHaHaHaHaHaHaHaHaHaHaHaHaHaHaHaHaHaHaHaH
aHa!
BAHAHAHAHAHAHAHAHAHAHAHAHAHAHAHAHAHAHA
HAHAHAHAHAHAHAHAHAHA!

[gasp]…

[snort].

MY TED TALK

I think if I am ever invited to give a TED Talk, I would talk about my vision of the future—what the world would look like in 50, 100, or 200 years from now.

For instance, in the not-too-distant future, we might have flying food. Nowadays, restaurateurs are already experimenting with robots and drones to deliver takeout orders to customers. What if there were flying donuts? You would just THINK of a donut flavor that you would like and a flying donut would automatically deliver itself to your home. Or, what about flying hot dogs? Same concept (although relish and onions might cause some aerodynamic issues). Although I have to admit I DO have my doubts about flying pork sandwiches. In my opinion, you'll see those when pigs fly.

Another great innovation will be indoor autonomous vehicles. Right now; Tesla, Google, and many of the automotive companies are developing autonomous vehicles to replace cars, trucks, buses, vans and sport utility vehicles. But I think, in the very distant future, we might have autonomous disk-shaped vehicles in the home that move from room-to-room providing transportation for your pets. For instance, your cat might want to ride on one of these disk vehicles. And, to make it extra useful, maybe it could vacuum the floors as it traveled around the house.

But I guess it will be a LONG time before we ACTUALLY see one of those.

MY FACEBOOK POWERS

AT LAST! I HAVE LEARNED TO USE MY FACEBOOK POWERS FOR GOOD!

Well… not GOOD…

Annoyance.

(But it's a GOOD annoyance.)

MIRACLE FABRIC

I think that someday, in the not-too-distant future, maybe even within my lifetime, they'll be able to take a 3D scan of my entire body from the neck down. Then they will be able to use that information to fabricate a set of clothes (maybe a onesie) that looked EXACTLY like my body. Then, when I put it on, I would look EXACTLY like I do when I'm naked—but (and here's the cool part)—I would be FULLY CLOTHED.

I think that would be a great thing but here's my biggest worry: I'm afraid that since I would LOOK naked, I might forget that I wasn't… and use the bathroom without removing my onesie. And then, I think…

That would ruin the whole effect.

MY THIRD HAIKU!

Just when you thought it was safe to look at your Facebook…

HAIKU! HAIKU! HAIKU! (Gesundheit)

For your reading displeasure, may I RESENT… HAIKU NUMBER 3:

Alliteration.
Seventeen syllables of
stupid silliness.

[bows quickly]

MY MEME

I sometimes think that if someone were to make a meme of me, it would probably be based around a concept something like:

IGNORANTLY CURIOUS or maybe CURIOUSLY IGNORANT.

But then I started thinking*… isn't curiosity ALWAYS caused by ignorance?

(And now I feel MUCH more less-dumber.)

*Yes. I had a thought.

MY VISION

People sometimes never ask me how I get ideas for my FaceBook posts. And I sometimes never say to them: It's not the finding of ideas that's key, it's the process. If you have a good process, the ideas will find you.

I have a guiding principle that can be best expressed as a metaphor. I think of myself as a literary treadmill. That is, when I sit down to write a post, my number-one goal is to lead you on a big round trip to nowhere and deposit you back where you were, sweating, nauseous and perhaps a little light-headed.

Of course, it's not the perfect metaphor, because when you get off a real treadmill, you will have improved a little bit as a person for having done it.

METEOROLOGIST INTERRUPTUS

My smartness phone just chirped and woke me up from my nap with this urgent message:

It's cloudy outside.

What am I supposed to do with THAT?

MAWAGE. MAWAGE IS WOT BWINGS US TOGEDDER TODAY.

If Mary Poppins married Poppin' Fresh…

She would be…

A BIG disappointment because she would become Mary Fresh which is a totally bland, uninteresting and DEFINITELY not-funny name. The world would be a lot cooler place if she could end up with a name like Poppin' Poppins, or Hoppity Poppity Poppins, or Poopin' Poppins (which was the kind of thing I was originally going for). But that's just not going to happen. She would end up with a totally unremarkable and tedious name—Mary Fresh—which sounds like a name of a totally dull, mundane, white bread, little girl from the suburbs whose most exciting life experience would be having to spend some time in detention because her lamb followed her to school one day.

So, ya. Kind of disheartening. But sometimes life gives you lemons and, try as you may, you just CAN'T quite make lemonade. All you can make is lemon juice…

Sour, repulsive, tart, acidic, hideous lemon juice.

Wait!

What if Mary Poppins married Mr. Popper's Penguins!??

Nope… I think not…

TOTALLY illegal in most states.

MOVIE REVIEW: PACIFIC RIM UPRISING

The wife, Nancy Matthews and I just got back from seeing Pacific Rim Uprising at the Emagine theater.

Full disclosure: we mostly went to experience the new Super Emax theater. The screen is 92 feet long and 48 feet tall. It's like going to a drive-in movie in the "old days" and sitting on the swing sets up up front. And they had a HUGE Dolby Atmos sound system. There must have been more than 200 speakers on all four walls and in several rows on the ceiling. I got a toothache from the intensity of the sound pressure alone! Talk about your basic FUN! I had a personal technology convulsion the moment we walked in. (Yes, in my case, that's a GOOD thing.)

And all the chairs are plush leather recliners—like so many powered Lazy Boy chairs. It felt like we were literally DUNKED in luxurious luxury.

The movie was fun. Of course, the plot was thin—but who goes to see a Pacific Rim movie expecting an elegant story arc?

Giant exoskeleton robots! Giant exoskeleton robots vs monsters—monsters that could easily gobble up Godzilla like a Flintstone vitamin!

THAT'S why you go!

MEATLESS DEATH

In order to improve my health, my new cardiologist told me to stop eating all animal products. So, I've given up all meat, fish, poultry, eggs, dairy, noses, hooves, etc. and started eating vegan hot dogs. Yes! HEALTHY vegan hot dogs. They actually MAKE healthy vegan hot dogs nowadays. You can BUY healthy vegan hot dogs!

And to prove to you that there are no animal products in them, here's the actual list of ingredients:

Water, soy protein isolate, soybean oil, evaporated cane syrup, pea protein isolate, tapioca starch, salt, potassium chloride, bakers yeast extract, carrageenan, dried garlic, natural flavor (from plant sources), natural smoke flavor, xanthan gum, fermented rice flour, guar gum, oleoresin paprika (color).

Okay…

You're right. In terms of health…

I'm not making any progress at all.

MICHIGAN WEATHER

Q: If April showers bring May flowers, what do April blizzards bring?

A: Despair.

MY MOST FAVORITIST THINGS

I think the jellyfish is one of nature's most AMAZING creatures. It's one of my MOST favoritist things. I mean they drift serenely along in the undulating ocean like little, lifeless, discarded, translucent plastic shopping bag fragments. Carried along, day-after-day, by the ocean currents, doing ABSOLUTELY nothing. Just drifting passively along like some piece of flotsamy ocean garbage. And when this lazy jellyfish just HAPPENS to drift into something else that is an ACTUAL, BONE FIDE, ACTIVE LIFE-FORM that actually thinks, feels, and MOVES on its own, this insipid, garbagey, drifter, shopping-bag-fragment-of-a-creature has the nerve to poison it with its stingy, dangly, slimy tentacles!

SEA BASTARD!!! YOU MAKE ME SOOOO MAD!!!!

Oh wait…

Did I say "Jellyfish"?

I meant, "Toast. With jelly."

THAT'S one of my MOST favoritist things.

MY INTERPLANETARY COLONIZATION HAIKU

Uranus rising.
Not your daily horoscope…
Colonoscopy.

MY COMPLEMENTS

Since I've been posting on Facebook, I've been getting a reputation as being "quite the deep thinker."

A couple of weeks ago, as I recall, some guy I HARDLY EVEN KNEW made a comment on one of my posts paying me the HIGHEST POSSIBLE complement. I mean, I don't remember EXACTLY what he said. And, sure, I guess I COULD look it up—but that would be too much like "research." And I guess we ALL know how little value there is in THAT. Anyway, he said something like, "You're really getting deep," or "IT'S really getting deep." Something like that. But… no matter.

Pretty sure those both mean about the same thing.

I GUESS I could look it up.

CHAPTER FOURTEEN
Nuns, Nikons, and Nakedness

NAKED, DUMB, AND AFRAID

I'm sorry. I don't care what the scientists tell us; we humans are NOT well equipped to survive on this planet. Scientists tell us we live on a "friendly", "hospitable" planet in the "Goldilocks Zone" where everything is perfect. If by the Goldilocks Zone they mean "in my air-conditioned house near a supermarket" then okay. If they mean "on earth with all the rest of those crawly, uncultured, odoriferous, wild, barely-scratching-out-a-living sentient beings"—I disagree. It is a FACT that mankind CANNOT survive unaided by technology in the wild. It's time to face the fact that we can only survive in MAN-MADE environments.

I mean, remember that time you went camping, and that moment you realized that you were on the verge of death because you were running low on Pringles? And it was 23 miles to the nearest camp store? What if your car had broken down? What if your party had been attacked by beavers... or OSTRICHES... or WILD, VENOMOUS, TURDUCKENS?!! What if (7-Eleven-Heaven forbid) the camp store was OUT OF PRINGLES?!!

DISASTER of course! Ultimate death, dismemberment, and DISASTER.

THAT'S what I'm talking about.

A while back (true story) we had a boil-water-advisory here in Oakland County (apparently the Russians had roofied our water or something), and we had to either buy bottled water or [gasp] BOIL OUR OWN WATER. And I thought to myself in horror: what if our stove breaks down at the EXACT same time that the store runs out of bottled water? We have ABSOLUTELY NO IDEA how to get water from acorns, or beveragefruit, or rivulets or WHEREVER you get water from in nature. We only know how to get water from a pipe (and those RUSSIAN DEVILS had taken that option away). All we could do was just lie down, put quarters on our eyes, and die.

Now some people LIKE to claim that we humans CAN live unaided in nature. And "they" always point to INDIGENOUS PEOPLE (from the Latin "INDE-GINUS" meaning "approaching death") as their prime example. The claim is that indigenous people can "live off the land"—hunting and gathering. "Hunting and gathering" is just a fancy anthropologist word for, "They do all their grocery shopping in the woods." Have you ever gone grocery shopping in the woods? Well, I have, and I can tell you… they're ALWAYS completely out of Pringles. And indigenous people KNOW this—they LIVE it daily. THAT'S why they look like that. Have you ever seen indigenous people? They're built like anorexic walking stick insects. And they only live until the age of nine. That's right. Maximum lifespan is nine-years-old. My DOG (who, incidentally, lives in a man-made environment) is older than that.

Yes. I know. I can hear it already, "But I've seen GAGGLES of 83-year-old indigenous women on the National Geographic channel sitting on the ground in circles beating yak meat on a rock."

No. They're INDIGENOUS! APPROACHING DEATH! They SHOP IN THE WOODS. They're not IN ACTUALITY FOR-REAL old. They only LOOK old. IN ACTUALITY FOR-REAL, those ALLEGED 83-year-old yak-meat-beating women are only middle school age! I'm TELLING you, living on earth is NOT easy!

THAT'S what I'm talking about.

Now, in order to study the capacity of humans to survive unaided in the wild, many scientific studies have been done—in the form of reality

TV shows. Have you SEEN these survival shows? These people are the survival EXPERTS. They are the ones that have access to the ENTIRE SUM of survival knowledge that we as a species have accrued. They are the VERY-TINY-SMALL percentage of the human race that have the ALLEGED skills to survive in the wild. And on these survival shows, they are deposited in serious, out-in-the-wild, survival situations and are MADE to "fish or cut the crap."

They are tasked with surviving in the wild for a total sum of three weeks. THREE WEEKS. That's it! Three weeks on their own. And many CAN'T DO IT! They GIVE UP. They CONCEDE! They quit early and go back to eating cheeseburgers. No blood—no foul.

And the ones that DO make it generally lose 20 to 30 pounds. 20 to 30 POUNDS! That's 10 POUNDS A WEEK. 500 POUNDS A YEAR! I don't know how many years of that the average human can take!

FRIENDLY ACQUAINTANCE: "Hey Bob! You look great! Looks like you lost a few pounds!"

ME: "Ya. I feel great! Would you believe it? I'm down about 1500. And I can FINALLY get back into that high school prom dress again!"

THAT'S what I'm talking about.

NAME THAT PLANET

Quickly. What do the following planet names have in common?

Mercury, Venus, Mars, Jupiter, Saturn, Uranus, Neptune.

If you guessed that all of the planet names were, in fact, NAMES OF PLANETS then; you are much like a lawyer—accurate but not helpful. If you guessed that they are all NOT EARTH, you win yourself an "I ❤ MOOSE FACTORY, ONTARIO" tote bag (thank you for playing). And if you guessed that they are all GODS, you get a WHOOP, WHOOP, ding, ding, ding… AND… you get to enter the BONUS ROUND!

Now, in my mind (such as it is), the coolest planet ever to exist was named after both a dog AND a Disney character. But THAT planet got kicked out of the solar system because it couldn't make weight*. "MUST BE 3.3 x 10^{23} kg TO RIDE." So, my point is that ALL of the planets, except for us (and the cast-off cartoon-canine stepplanet), were named after GODS. GODS!

OUR planet, on the other hand, was named after DIRT…

Not cool.

*All you Bill Nye science nerd guys out there: I know I've caused you GREAT ANXIETY but don't get your leptons all in a bunch! Please don't send me your "weight vs mass dissertation." Just LET IT GO! RELAX. Go have a big bowl of Lucky Charms and another energy drink… Deep breaths… That's right…

NUT TIGHTENING

Whitie tighty…

Lefty loosie

NET WORTHLESS

I saw yesterday that Mark Zuckerberg has 94,728,641 followers on Facebook.

I have FOUR.

And I think you'd probably get about the SAME RATIO…

If you compared our net-worths.

NAKED, AFRAID, AND SMART

I'm not a regular watcher, but I've seen NAKED AND AFRAID several times now because who DOESN'T like to watch starving, terrified, nude people argue with each other for 42 minutes every week?

So, I guess one of the stipulations of the show is that the naked folks are allowed to bring ONE THING with them to help them survive their few weeks of fun and merriment. They usually bring some kind of fundamental survivor thing like a knife, a fire-starter, a metal cup, or a linear particle accelerator.

Now, I've given this a LOT of thought. And I think if I were to be on NAKED AND AFRAID, I'd bring a cow.

Now, you probably think I'd slaughter it on DAY ONE and start eating the meat right away. But I wouldn't. I'm too smart for that.

I'd keep it around the first few days and just eat the milk and eggs.

NOT AGAIN!!!

You know that TV show that my wife likes—that women's "talk" show where Whoopi Goldberg, Joy Behar and a throng of various other millionaire women argue AND try to out-yell each other for a full 42 minutes EVERY DAY?

I think when it goes into reruns, they should call it DEJA VIEW.

NIKON D810 DSLR

ME: I absolutely LOVE my Nikon D810 DSLR camera! I've owned

many cameras over my lifetime and this is BY FAR, the most PERFECT camera ever. To begin with, it feels great in my hands with a big, meaty grip that allows me to hold it comfortably and securely. It's got a full-frame 36 MP sensor, excellent low-light performance, and a very impressive dynamic range. It's very durable with a weatherproof magnesium body. It will shoot up to 5 frames-per-second in continuous mode and it has a very fast and sophisticated autofocus system.

I can talk about technical specs all day, but the fact is it takes AMAZING photos. In short, the Nikon D810 is PERFECT in every way. This is a camera that CAN NOT POSSIBLY be improved upon. It is, by far, the most incredible camera I've ever laid my hands on. I can't express it any stronger than this:

THIS IS PROBABLY THE LAST CAMERA I WILL EVER NEED TO BUY.

NIKON: We've just announced the release of our next generation camera—the D850.

ME: Oooooooo! I want this!

NEEDY

Better to have and not need, than to need and not have needed again.

NANCY AND THE PIRATE

I think my wife, Nancy, and the Dread Pirate Roberts are the same person because…

I've NEVER SEEN THEM TOGETHER…

And they sometimes wear similar hats.

NUN SENSE

I have always wondered if nuns sort their clothing into good habits and bad habits.

NORMAL

WIFE: You've been acting a little strange lately.

ME: How so?

WIFE: You know. You've been acting really odd… kinda off-the-wall… saying goofy things… just WEIRD, I suppose.

ME: Different than normal?

[pause]

WIFE: Forget I mentioned it.

NAME A GAME THE WHOLE FAMILY CAN PLAY!

He tried very hard to get his sister to go out on a date with him.

In fact, some would say he was quite incestant.

Go ahead—laugh. It's okay. You KNOW YOU WANT TO.

(And, just to be clear: I personally, am an ONLY CHILD.)

NO MOVEMENT

THE CONSTIPATION NAZI: No poop for YOU!!!

(Definitely NOT Trotsky)

CHAPTER FIFTEEN
Opinions, Outcasts, and Oppenheimerland

OFF-THE-JOB TRAINING

As a small child in pre-revolutionary France being groomed as a future executioner; I wonder if your mom was always yelling at you:

"DON'T RUN WITH THAT GUILLOTINE!"

OPRY FACTS

So, my wife and I just went to a show at the Grand Ole Opry. And my wife, Nancy Matthews (whom, due to her standing subscription to People Magazine is a Hollywood and Nashville expert), gave me some interesting facts:

Apparently, Keith Urban is married to Nichol Kiddman who is apparently ALSO married to Tom Cruise who is apparently also married to L. Ron Hubbard who is the child of space aliens.

And I know this for a fact because I always listen very carefully to my wife.

OUR LEGACY

Why do we do it—disclose little mundane bits of our lives online? Photos of us eating gummy bears with chopsticks, beating balloon animals with a golf club or farting into a campfire? When we make a Facebook, we make a decision to live at least a part of our lives publicly. Why do we do it?

I believe we do it because we see it as our only shot at immortality. It is a way to be remembered. It is our legacy. We all know we are inevitably headed for that big landfill in the sky. But perhaps, if we leave a bit of our lives behind, some PART of us will survive. Our Facebook serves as EVIDENCE that we were here.

I dream that someday, millions of millenniums from now, after homo not-as-sapiens-as-they-thought-they-were has vanished from the planet; some cockroach archaeologist will find some piece of intact, functioning media with my Facebook posts on it. And the cockroach archaeologist will play it for its fellow colleagues. And they will remark to each other,

“No wonder they're extinct!”

And I will have my own little piece of immortality.

OUTCAST

What if the whole world suddenly ENDED, but you were in the bathroom, so you missed it?

Would you feel left out?

OUTLYING

People who are REAL professional writers outline EVERYTHING they write ahead of time so that their works are congruent and coherent. They CLAIM that an outline keeps them well-organized and on track all the way through their… um… thing-that-they’re-writing.

Now, that's fine for some, but I personally, don't believe in outlining. It takes too much time and it ruins my spontaneity, and…

HEY LOOK! A SQUIRREL!!!

And… Uhhh…

And THAT'S… why we can't have nice things!

Anymore…

Did I mention I don't outline?

ODD ODDS

Here's an interesting fact:

Out of all of the many hundreds—even THOUSANDS—of people I've met, none of them have EVER been ME. None. Not even ONE! I'm the only one that I've EVER met that's been me.

What are the odds?

OPINIONS

Opinions are like Uranus.

Every astronaut has one.

OPPENHEIMERLAND

Little 6-year-old Bobby Oppenheimer had thirteen stars on the original flag he designed for his new nation that he was founding—Oppenheimerland. They were the thirteen gold stars his third-grade teacher, Mrs. Heimenopper had awarded him for various scientific achievements in class. Most notable was his third-grade science fair project—a model of a volcano cleverly fashioned entirely from cookie dough, construction paper, duct tape, two button-holes, some toilet paper rolls, vinegar, baking soda, and 23 emergency road flares.

However, little Bobby never got to fly his nation's colors because Mrs. Heimenopper decided to take back all the stars and abolish the young, sovereign nation…

When predictably, Oppenheimerland got "the bomb."

ONLINE BANKERING

I like online bankering. I can just go online, log into my credit card accounts and use my Visa to pay off my American Express card. I can then use my American Express card to settle my Visa account. Now, with both credit card accounts paid off in full…

I have absolutely NO WORRIES.

And I didn't even have to lick any envelopes.

CHAPTER SIXTEEN
Pigs, Planking, and Pluto

PLEASANT DREAMS

I rarely remember dreams but I remember a couple from last night. In one of them, a friend of mine was sitting cross-legged on the ground. I jumped up in the air effortlessly, and circled him while floating and executing five perfect karate kicks without making contact—all the while wearing heavy hiking boots… just because. At the end of it, I hovered for a few tenths of a second in front of him and then put my feet down. It was totally Matrixy.

Of course, everyone (in the dream) was amazed. I just gave them a little smile (you know that coy little Mona Lisa smile I'm known for) and acted like, "Ya. I do that all the time."

In the other dream, a bunch of us were being held captive in an old house and being picked off one-by-one. I was the only one left in the room and a guy was coming up the stairs for me. I watched him through a crack in the door and... (also through sheer curtains. What's up with that?) When he entered the room, I jumped out and punched him dead in the face. The punch had all the impact of two spacecraft gently docking. (My punches never work in my dreams.) Then I lapel-grabbed him by the shirt and threw him through a glass window. He plunged to his death on the well-manicured front lawn.

Gotta admit, it's kinda fun killing bad guys and levitating at will. But I also gotta say, real life is pretty good too.

BTW: Happy 4th of July America!

PROTECTING MY FAMILY

When my daughter, Kristen, was just a little girl in kindergarten, she asked if our family could please go to Disney World. I told her that just to be safe, our family should probably stay home…

Because the hunter that killed Bambi's mother was still at large.

PLANKING

The older I get, the more the idea of bringing back PLANKING sounds like a good one.

Because…

LYING DOWN…

Anywhere.

[lying down]

PERKS

I think if you were in the army in the Middle Ages and you were the catapult guy, I feel like it would be a REALLY FUN THING if they let you bring the catapult home on weekends.

But then, it would ALSO be a BURDEN because all of your neighbors would want to join in on the fun. And they'd CONSTANTLY be hounding you to launch their old sofas, dirty dishes, saltwater aquariums, small children—stuff like that—into the next village.

PHONES

I sometimes see people get upset because they forgot their phone at home. They'll say things like,

"Dang flappit! I left my fram farkin phone at home!"

That's how you know they're miffed.

I remember, way back last century when leaving your phone at home was pretty much the NORM. We always left our phones at home because, back in those days, your phone didn't work unless it had a house plugged into it. If somehow, your house got unplugged from your phone, your phone stopped working. That was just the way it was. So, we never took the phone outside unless we felt like swinging it in big circles around our head by the cord (which I found out the hard way; my father did NOT condone).

Nowadays, if you see someone you know ACROSS THE WAY that you want to talk to, you can just ring them up on your phone and have a chat. Back in the day, we didn't do that because you had to go home to use the phone. And if for some reason, you decided you just HAD to go home to make that call, they wouldn't answer—because they weren't home. YOU JUST SAW THEM OUTSIDE! IDIOT! Furthermore, you could try leaving a message, but that was almost always ineffective because we didn't have answering machines either. So, the phone just rang UNTIL THE COWS CAME HOME which meant FOREVER, because we also didn't have cows.

So, when we saw someone across the way that we wanted to talk to, we used to use an old-school technique that I like to call "yelling." Then the other person would either yell back or wave (not to be confused with "the wave" which is a baseball stadium audience participation activity that we also didn't have).

Nowadays, some people call these old-style phone LAND LINES. Back then, we just called them "phones." And I think LAND LINES is an odd thing to call them because they had nothing to do with THE LAND. In fact, the phone company did all it could to keep the telephone wires from even touching THE LAND. They used to erect tall wooden poles and carefully string the wires from pole to pole—all the way from the telephone company to your house to make sure the wires didn't touch the ground. Because if the wires DID happen to touch the ground such as any time they were subjected to a gust of wind stronger than a bee fart; your phone would stop working.

This made for an annoying state of affairs. On nice days, your phone would work, but you would be outside (because that's what we used to do on nice days) so you WOULDN'T talk on it. On inclement days, you would be forced to stay inside near the phone, which didn't work (because of the bee-fart wind gusts) so you COULDN'T talk on it.

So, as I said, land lines had absolutely nothing to do with the land. It was all about having a house plugged into them. So, I guess we maybe we should call them HOUSE PHONES…

But for some reason, HOUSE PHONES always seem to have HOTELS plugged into them.

PERSEID PERILS

The story you are about to read is true. Only MY name hasn't been changed to protect the innocent:

I've been spending a fair amount of time staring up at the sky lately. Most recently we had the TOTAL PARTIAL (79%) solar eclipse here in Michigan and then, just a little over a week ago, we had the 2017 edition of the annual Perseid Meteor Shower. I thought "the Perseid" would be kind of a cool thing to see because: Hey! Flaming balls of fire in the sky! (They say if you listen carefully you can hear them scream.)

No… Wait… That's LOBSTERS.

So, Friday night, a little before midnight, I dragged a chaise lounge out near the street, reclined back, and watched. It was not long, maybe 45 minutes-to-an-hour before the real excitement started. And by EXCITEMENT, I mean the kind of excitement that has absolutely NOTHING to do with flaming celestial fireballs.

I noticed two sets of headlights coming down the street. The first SUV slowed down as it passed by me and stopped several feet to my left. I could tell by the roof-mounted red and blue light-bar that this was NO ORDINARY SUV. The second SUV came to a stop to my right with all of its lights trained on me. And this was just seconds before the THIRD SUV pulled up from my left and stopped on my left. All three SUVs arrived within seconds of each other—just as if they had some kind of magical, incomprehensible way of communicating with each other!

So, there I was; 12:30 at night—a sixty-something, white-haired old man; wearing basketball shorts, a T-shirt, and sandals, on my front lawn, lying prone on a chaise lounge, surrounded by THREE OAKLAND COUNTY SHERIFFS who were collectively training enough law-enforcement candlepower on me to make me look like my own personal shopping mall grand opening. I tentatively checked my torso for red laser spots.

We, of course, had a short discussion about the nature of my scientific, supine, shooting-star, sky-survey. And at the end of our brief discussion, the officer remarked, "Sorry to bother you. It's just that SOME OF YOUR NEIGHBORS WERE WORRIED ABOUT YOU."

Now, to be fair, these guys were pretty cool about the whole thing. And I'm grateful to have them "out there" protecting our community from people like me. But I just can't imagine the various conversations that had to have happened in order to have brought us all to this point. (Full disclosure: Actually, I CAN imagine the conversations that had to have happened in order to have brought us all to this point and I'm going to make them up right now).

“Tarnation Leonard! Look there's an old man out there on the Matthews' lawn... and he's laying on something... LAWN FURNITURE I think! Might even be COMMUNIST CHINESE lawn furniture!”

“Jumpin' encephalitis Gwendolyn! You've hit the zipper right on the button! Looks like a gangster... or... basketball player or... a whaddaycallit... TERRORIST!”

“Well raise my rent and call me 'Brangelina', Leonard! I've heard tell of these types of BASTARDITOS! They recline in chaise lounges in plain view of your house so that they can see when you're not looking at them. Then, they break into your home, eat your leftovers, erase your DVR, unload the dishwasher and run down the road chortling. HOLY MENSTRUAL CRAMPS LEONARD! We better call the Alcohol, Tobacco and Lawn Furniture Bureau—and PRONTO!”

BOOP BOOP. BEEP. BOOP BOOP. BIP BOOP BOOP.
Ring ring ring ring ring…

“Hello, Oakland County Sheriff's Office. Sgt. Yemana speaking. How may I help you?”

“There's a man layin out on our neighbor, Bob Matthews' lawn. Whadaya gonna do about it?”

“Can you describe him Mam?”

“Well… he looks kinda like Bob Matthews… but not quite.”

“Is it POSSIBLE that it might just BE Bob Matthews, Mam?”

“I don't know. He's wearing… well, I didn't want to mention it over an unsecure phone, but… he wearing BASKETBALL SHORTS."

"BASKETBALL SHORTS! WHY DIDN'T YOU SAY SO? We'll send EVERY AVAILABLE UNIT RIGHT AWAY!"

So. To reiterate: The story you have just heard IS true (really). The names have been changed to protect the IDIOTS and ALSO because I have ABSOLUTELY NO IDEA who called the FREAKIN' COPS ON ME! And one last thing (and this is ALSO absolutely true):

As they were leaving, I noticed that one of the officers had "K-9" embroidered on the front of his uniform. So, although I didn't actually SEE it, what I think that means is...

They ALSO sent a FREAKIN' ATTACK DOG!

PIGS HOPING TO FLY

You've heard me say it before: Baby robins eat fourteen feet of earthworms each and every day.

Here's an idea: How about NOT eating them?

It seems to me that they might want to stop eating for a day or two and save up those worms. Then, they could tie them together like bedsheets in a hotel fire and shimmy down to the ground thereby avoiding that risky, sometimes-fatal, first attempt at flight.

But NOOOOO. They'll probably just eat them.

Birdbrains.

PAINED FACES

You know those PAIN SCALE diagrams you see at the doctor's office or at the hospital? Those small wall posters that have little cartoon heads that go from comfort-to-agony in six easy steps?

Apparently, you're supposed to pick out the one that most reflects what you're currently feeling in your own little personal cartoon body and point at it like a two-year-old. You've seen those diagrams, right? Well, that's not what I want to talk about. What I WANT to talk about is this:

I think they should have one of those charts for DRUNKENNESS. Of course, it would never work because drunk people are in no condition to make reliable judgments. Nor can they see clearly, point at ANYTHING in particular, nor say the words bishshastio* or buhshetti**. But hey! THINK of the FACES!

It would make going to the hospital FUN again!

*pistachio
**spaghetti

PRESIDENTIAL SWEET

I wonder. If the US government decided to adopt one of those increasingly-popular open office concepts…

Would the president have to sit in the "Oval Cubicle"?

PEOPLE!!!

"PEOPLE" sometimes say to me: May all your dreams come true.

But what if I dreamt that I was being chased by a herd of barbarous, enraged, giant, robot ostriches shooting laser-guided hornets at me and I couldn't run because my legs were awkward, beefy, uncontrollable, unresponsive stumps that barely moved no matter how much effort I expended and I was simultaneously being attacked from the sky by flying, Nazi, mutant, mythical half-woodchuck/half-octopus creatures who rained down a lethal flood of claw hammers and brimstone (claw hammers and brimstone!!!) and the ground began to crumble beneath my feet in huge chunks and fall away into a great pit of vipers, spiders, and bears (oh my!) and as the laser-guided hornets, claw hammers and brimstone zinged past my head, I was being run down from behind by a colossal, roaring, raging wall of fire, smoke, poison gas, Rottweilers, Rototillers, Vikings, Visigoths, locusts, and stampeding Amway salesmen?

What then? Huh?!!

Bite me "PEOPLE."

PROGRESS

200,000 years ago, homo sapiens was a primitive, wholly unremarkable creature who spent most of the waking day simply endeavoring to survive. Life was tenuous, difficult and perilous for early mankind. It was not uncommon to have to walk dozens of miles to obtain water to make mud, or to have to rub two rocks together—sometimes for days—to create the necessary amount of rock dust. But as sapiens better adapted to their environment, they began to use their relatively GIANT BRAINS to innovate and increase their chances for survival as a species.

A pivotal point was reached on one momentous morning, when a solitary sapiens man or women arose and, unwittingly, over a period of several hours, stitched together hundreds of field mouse pelts to make the first pair of Capri pants (back then they were called "pedal-pushers")—and the technology revolution was launched. Flash forward a couple of millenniums later and we have the coat-hanger, the soap-dish, and the Popeil Pocket Fisherman. And it gets better!

If I want to—without even getting out of my chair—I can yell "ALEXA! PULL MY FINGER!" from anywhere in the house and a shameless, flatulent, resounding fart noise will resonate from my kitchen.

And that's JUST AN EXAMPLE of how far we've come in the last 200,000 years.

PHOTO OP

I went Thanksgiving grocery shopping today at my friendly neighborhood Kroger supermarket (which Google, by way of my smartness phone, informed me was a popular photo opportunity).

I'm planning on hiring a photographer and coming back tomorrow.

PENNY FOOLISH

What do we need pennies for? Have you ever considered just how LITTLE a penny is worth? Have you ever THOUGHT about what you can actually BUY for a penny? Well, I have, and you're going to have to get your microscope out for this one.

You can buy EXACTLY .0208 of an ounce of a Snickers Bar. TWO-ONE HUNDREDTHS of an OUNCE of a Snickers Bar! Basically, that's a piece of SNICKERS DUST. Let me help you picture that:

Say, for example, that you and I were lost at sea and hadn't eaten for days. And you—YOU BASTARD! —were gnashing away on our last Snickers bar and you would stubbornly REFUSE to share! And I would try and grab at that candy bar in your grimy, smutty paw; but you would keep pushing me away with your wrinkly, soggy, squalid foot as you gnawed on our final fistful of foodstuffs. And then I would grab you and, hysterically clutching each other, we would recklessly roll about the floor of the rubber raft (did I mention we were in a rubber raft?) locked in a violent, desperate scuffle for raft domination—battling in the rain (by the way, it's also raining)—over the last few meager, nourishing bites of candy bar. And when you had finally gotten down to the last two-one hundredths of an ounce, you would maybe suffer a slight change of heart and offer this last one-penny's-worth of candy to me. And even though I was starving and was going to die; I'd weakly flick the back of my hand at you and retort…

"Pfffff. Why bother? Forget it."

And then I'd try to kill you.

THAT'S how little a penny is worth.

PHONE PHRUSTRATION

Siri. What's the weather like in Petoskey, Michigan?

[silence]

Siri—the weather?

[silence]

SIRI!??? WHAT'S THE WEATHER?!!! THE WEEEEATHERRRR!!!

[silence]

Damn Android phone.

PREDICTIVE GPS?

I think I've got a predictive GPS.

When I miss my turn, my GPS tells me to make a U-turn.

“When possible… Please make a U-turn,” she says.

My GPS just told me to make an O-turn. How did she KNOW I was going to miss my turn twice?

PICTURE THIS

For centuries on end, men nearly as wise as me have pondered the worth of words. And now, I alone, am ready to reveal the answer to all of humanity:

Each word is worth exactly one millipicture.

(Do the math.)

PLUTO? GONE.

Well, Pluto is gone. We all know that. And when I say it's “gone”, I mean it's still out there. But it's been demoted. I guess the International Interstellar Solar Planet Institution or whatever other “official” pompous, elitist organization that gets to say who's a planet and who's not, figured that it didn't meet their height requirement (You Must Be This Tall to Ride This Solar System). In spite of this, I'm sure Pluto's doing okay—way out there—still happily circling (ellipticaling?) around. In fact, it probably doesn't care—probably hasn't even gotten the news yet.

But things are different here on earth. Many of us are still DARN upset about the demotion. ALL THOSE YEARS, it was—and then suddenly—it isn't. And here's the interesting thing:

We Americans are pretty much alone on this. Most of the world doesn't give a flying-bacon-rasher about Pluto. When told Pluto had been demoted, most of the world responded with, “Pass the ketchup please." But here in America, we were FURIOUS.

I read that the reason that Americans are primarily the only ones upset by this planetary demotion is that we Americans absolutely LOVE Pluto—not the planet—the DOG. Here in the US, we all grew up with Disney's lovable, rambunctious, yellow animated canine—and we learned to love him. In Europe, they grew up with Lamborghinis, French wine, and Italian supermodels. So ya.

"Yellow canine cartoon? I fart at your yellow canine cartoon!"

So, I guess the operative principle here is: If something is basically just a rock to us—drifting somewhere out in space—who cares? But if it's something we grew up with all of our lives—something near and dear to us—something we're VERY attached to; DON'T MESS WITH IT.

So, with that in mind, you know who's NEVER going to get demoted?

Uranus.

PARENTING MEMORIES

My kids are grownups now, but I remember them fondly when they were still little tykes—back in the days before they could walk. They would spend their ENTIRE day crawling around on the floor. They were so cute.

And that was a VERY good age—because you could ride them around the living room. Sure, they weren't very fast…

But I used to LOVE the little noises they made.

PRIORITIES

I actually think it's a good idea to HAVE priorities.

I just think it's WAY too much trouble to put them in order.

POT CALLING THE KETTLE STRIPED

There are over seven and a half billion people on the planet. And yet, hardly anyone ever eats humans anymore.

Oh sure, occasionally a shark or a bear nabs some poor, unsuspecting touristy person and munches on them a bit. But, in general, we have no natural predators and our population is growing—essentially unchecked.

So, it kinda makes you wonder why we're making such a big deal over the zebra mussel. Doesn't it?

PLEASED

Have you noticed? Today, absolutely no one refers to excrement as "caca" anymore. No one EVER uses that word. It seems to have fallen into disuse.

That pleases me.

PATRIOTISM

I don't know much about politics. All I know is that it's really kinda interesting that our president was named after some of America's landmarks… towers… buildings… skyscrapers… those kinds of things.

Seems kind of patriotic somehow.

PASTRY FACE

ME: See? This balaclava isn't so bad. I mean, sure—it's a little chewy. And it's got a little bit of a rubbery taste. I think maybe next time maybe we don't get the neoprene one. Maybe next time we should get the fleece one or the cloth one.

THE WIFE: Next time? NEXT TIME??!!! There will BE NO NEXT TIME!!! Listen to this and listen CAREFULLY!!!

THIS was absolutely the last time I'm EVER sending YOU out to buy the BAKLAVA!!! IDIOT!!!

Now pass those scissors over here!

PORNTIFICATING

When "actors" have staged, orchestrated "relations" in adult movies, I think they should call it "pornicating."

(See what I did there?)

PROBLEMS

If your only tool is a hammer…

Then every problem looks like a thumb.

PUBLIC SERVICE

People sometimes never ask me why I spend so much time writing these posts. And my answer is that I do it as a public service. It keeps me occupied. If I wasn't sitting in front of my computer composing and publishing these posts, I'd have to go find something else to do. And if you don't agree with me that writing these posts is a valuable public service, ask yourself this simple question:

Would you RATHER have me behind the wheel of a 4000-lb car…

Careening down the road at YOU?

"No further questions, Your Honor."

PULP FICTION

Establishing shot of a smallish, nondescript room. Two sheets of blank printer paper lie on a table adjacent to each other. Camera zooms in to reveal that one of the pieces of paper has a small, precise cut on its upper edge. After a slight pause, cut to medium shot of the two pieces of paper conversing.

PAPER ONE: I notice you have a little cut there on the top of your head. What happened?

PAPER TWO: Oh that. You know… that little girl… scissors.

PAPER ONE: Ya. Of course. Does it hurt?

PAPER TWO: YES! It's EXCRUCIATING. Have you noticed?!! NOTHING seems to hurt like one of those nasty little people-cuts. Can you THINK of anything worse?

PAPER ONE: Spit wads.

PAPER TWO: Oh ya. I hear THAT. SPIT wads. Spit wads and origami. I HATE origami! That reminds me… gotta get to my chiropractor soon.

Fade to black.

"CUT!!!"

PROGENITORIA

When you stop to think about it, it was not really THAT long ago, that MY ancestors all used to live up in the TREES…

Until the police threw them out of the park.

CHAPTER SEVENTEEN
Reality, Regret, and Reredundancy

RUBBING IT IN YOUR FACEBOOK

Yay! I did it! I'm ACTUALLY on Facebook!

Mark Zuckerberg must be PISSED.

ROLLING BOIL

Apparently, a watched pot DOES boil…

(But only when you're NOT looking at it).

REALITY (VS.) TV

I wonder: If someone produced a reality show that was ACTUALLY BASED ON REALITY…

Would anyone watch it?

RUE THE DAY

I think the phrase "rue the day" has become exceedingly underutilized. So, I've decided I'm bringing back "rue the day." Here, for your perusal and reading pleasure, is my very first utilization:

You will rue the day you accepted my friend request.

REREDUNDANT

Flammable… Inflammable…

One of those words seems INNECESSARY.

ROLE REVERSAL

Imagine if dogs owned us instead of the other way around. I mean sure, we would lose some of our freedoms. But think of the advantages.

WE wouldn't need jobs. THEY would do that. WE could sleep a lot because basically, that would be our job. And THEY would be responsible for feeding US. And WE wouldn't even have to wear clothes—but THEY would. WE wouldn't have to make our own decisions. Our DOGS would do that for us. This alone could save us from LOADS of embarrassing incidents. For instance:

Say my dog (let's call her "Liz") took me out for "walkies" and we were trotting down the street and we saw another dog who was out walking the beautiful human woman she owned; and I immediately started tugging against my leash because I REALLY, URGENTLY wanted to rush right over and sniff this beautiful woman's butt—and not just one of those polite, demure little sniffs that one might use to sniff a butterfly's face—but one of those long, protracted, staccato series of aggressive, wet-nosed, air-blast sniffs that makes a woman start to get that "Hey! What's going ON back there?!!" sort of feeling; Liz would sharply yank on my leash and say, "No no," to save me from performing this embarrassing, carnal act.

Then Liz would pat me on the head and say, "Good boy," as I proudly squatted and pooped on the neighbor's lawn.

[Sigh]

What a wonderful world THAT would be.

RANDOM "FACTS" REGARDING THE MAYOR OF Bob's WoRld

You know those dumb quizzes "they" post on Facebook in order to insidiously extract all kinds of secret, personal information from gullible ignoramuses so that "they" can hack into all of those pea-brain-idiots' online accounts and STEAL all of the online-account-stuff from those block-headed numbskulls?

Here's an ACTUAL Facebook survey that I filled out. The questions are "theirs". The answers are INDISPUTABLY mine:

Q: Do you make your bed every day?
A: Yes. And if I have time, I also build a dresser.

Q: What's your favorite number?
A: -ish

Q: What is your job?
A: I don't HAVE a job. I'm just that old guy at McDonald's who yells obscenities at the drive-thru guy and never orders anything more than a senior coffee.

Q: If you could, would you go back to school?
A: I can. I would. I don't.

Q: Can you parallel park?
A: As I look outside, my car looks PERFECTLY parallel with my driveway. So… YES.

Q: Name a job you had which people would be shocked to know you had.
A: I used to "work" in the WalMart lingerie department—until SECURITY noticed.

Q: Do you think aliens exist?
A: Yes—and boy am I homesick!

Q: Can you drive a stick shift?
A: Yes, but I'd rather drive a car.

Q: Guilty pleasure?
A: I believe I may have already mentioned the WalMart lingerie department.

Q: Favorite childhood game?
A: Cowboys and waitresses.

Q: Do you talk to yourself?
A: Nope. The voices in my head do that for me.

Q: Do you like doing puzzles?
A: Nope. I find them to be too… (what's the word I'm looking for?) … puzzling.

Q: Favorite music?
A: Metal. (My feeling is that REALLY good music should injure you).

Q: Coffee or tea?
A: PAY ATTENTION!!! #@$%@&&@!!!! I SAID SENIOR COFFEE!!!!

Q: First thing you remember you wanted to be when you grew up?
A: Swedish.

Q: Favorite Season?
A: Breaking Bad Season 4—in which Gus (spoiler alert) goes to the big meth lab in the sky.

Q: Truck or Car?
A: Minivan (because my wife bought it for me and assured me it would be the perfect "chick-magnet").

Q: Steak or Salad?
A: I'm from the planet Vegan.

Q: Cat or dog?
A: Dog. Cats swear too much. What's up with that?

Q: The most influential person from your childhood?
A: I'll always remember the advice Gort—the robot from THE DAY THE EARTH STOOD STILL gave to me. "Klaatu barada nikto," he said.

Q: Crafty or all thumbs?
A: I have VERY crafty thumbs.

Q: Biggest fear?
A: Fear itself.

Q: Pessimist or Optimist?
A: Engineer.

Q: Favorite Holiday?
A: Doc. No, wait! Billie… Yes… Billie.

Q: Mountains or Ocean?
A: I have both.

Q: People person?
A: Trick question! (Those two are the SAME THING).

Q: White, Milk or Dark Chocolate?
A: Bacon rinds.

Q: Do you like to cook?
A: I like to "work" in the WalMart lingerie department (pro bono).

Q: Night owl or morning person?
A: Afternoon delight.

Q: Flannel sheets in winter?
A: Nope. Plaid makes me look too much like a giant bagpipe!

REGRET

Have you ever been going about your normal day—doing your normal everyday stuff? Maybe it's after lunch—in the middle of the day. Maybe you've been in meetings or been out shopping or you just finished lunch with a group of friends.

And you come out of the bathroom and you happen to pass a full-length mirror and see yourself for the first time today and wonder to yourself…

Who the HELL was the deranged, psychopath that DRESSED this person?!!

(Or… maybe the enchanted bluebirds and mice that dressed you this morning were hungover.)

REJOICE!

Dance like there WAS NO YESTERDAY!

REAL MUSIC

I went to the gym today to listen to music on headphones. My playlist included: Metallica, Slipknot, Iced earth, Iron maiden, Dream Theater,

Circus Maximus, and Avenged Sevenfold. Most of you who have known me for more than a short time, know my philosophy on music:

REALLY good music should injure you.

If it doesn't do PERMANENT damage to the central nervous system, feel free to play it in your elevator or on your phone system while you've got me on hold waiting to be connected to your technical support dweebs in Siam. It's not like I'm going to listen to it anyway.

Also, while I was there at the gym, (remember the gym?) I lifted some weights.

REAL TRUTH

REAL TRUTH is NOT about opinions, rumors, hearsay or hunches.

REAL TRUTH is about evidence-based FACTS. It's about things you can SEE. Things you can TOUCH. Things you can TASTE. Things you can SMELL. And things you can HEAR—ESPECIALLY the things the VOICES in your head tell you… over and over… REPEATEDLY… RELENTLESSLY… almost until you CAN'T STAND IT!!!

Everything else is unreliable.

CHAPTER EIGHTEEN
Sofa Beds, Science, and Sprit Animals

SHOELESS IN SEATTLE

I cried because I had no shoes, until I met a man who had no feet...

So, I took his shoes.

NOW, who's crying?

SHHHH

When I was a little boy, I used to walk four miles back and forth to school, through the snow, with no coat, no boots, no gloves…

Till mom found out.

STANDARD DEVIATIONS

I think a really successful dating book would be one that simply teaches men how to identify women with low standards.

SPACE SHOT

The privatization of the space exploration industry has radically altered the US spaceflight landscape. And of course, SpaceX has emerged as one of the leading players in the space exploration game.

SpaceX has shown itself to be a very innovative and creative company. I think a great name for one of their future devices for shooting people into space would be…

(wait for it…)

The Elon Musket.

STAY TUNED

There is more than enough disappointment in this life to go around. If there isn't…

I will create more tomorrow.

SKINNY TEETH?

HE MADE IT BY THE SKIN OF HIS TEETH.

What does that even MEAN?

She made it by the enamel of her eyeballs.

He made it by the roots of his hairnails.

She made it by her foot-cheeks.

See what I mean?

Sorry. Didn't mean to rant. It was just a SPEEN-JERK reaction.

I'm gonna quit now.

I think I'm getting a BRAIN CRAMP.

STRAIGHT FROM THE HORSE'S MOUTH

When people tell me they got something STRAIGHT FROM THE

HORSE'S MOUTH, I tell them I'm not touching it until they at least rinse it off.

SENSELESS BUREAU

According to the US Census Bureau, which I am TEMPTED to refer to as the "US Senseless Bureau"—not because I am an informed person that knows even the FIRST THING about them—but simply because it happens to be part of the US government. But, although I'm TEMPTED to call them this, I am careful NOT to actually to refer to them in this manner because A) I tend to be exceedingly respectful and fearful of ANYONE in the US Government because they have co-workers that have the ability to drop a smart bomb into my personal underwear drawer—from SPACE! and B) I'm sure it's staffed with some very fine people (the Bureau, not the smart bomb) who are really good at counting stuff.

But anyway, according to them (and this part is POSITIVELY true), a child is BORN in the US every eight seconds and a person DIES every 12 seconds. So, we can only HOPE that at the EXACT 24-second mark…

The person who drops dead is NOT the doctor who happens to be delivering the baby who is being born.

Because: statistics.

SAMSNUG SPELLUNG

Hey! Quick question: Do any of you Samsung Galaxy S8 ushers out there know how to turn off autocarrot?

SCIENCE SEMINAR

Someday I'd like to visit a people so primitive, so remote, so backward... that they've never even SEEN dry ice. And then I'd tell them EVERYTHING about it—about how it works, how it looks, and how it's ICE… but it's DRY.

But first, I'd have to bone up on dry ice. Because how do they DO that? And all that smoke! What's THAT about? Does that stuff have FIRE in it?

SNEAKY STEALTH SPACE STORM FROM SPACE!

This just in from OFFICIAL SPACE SCIENTIST PEOPLE: A space storm could hit the earth at ANY MOMENT and we would only have 15 minutes notice. That's right! Kinda like a SNEAKY STEALTH SPACE STORM FROM SPACE!

The consequences could be DEVASTATING for our planet! The OFFICIAL SPACE SCIENTIST PEOPLE are predicting that Facebook and Twitter could be down for DAYS or more!

The worst possible kind of space storm that could hit us would be a Coronal Mass Injection (which, besides being a calamitous, disastrous space-weather event would ALSO be a very cool band name). OFFICIAL SPACE SCIENTIST PEOPLE tell us that a Coronal Mass Injection (which I think could ALSO be some kind of intravenous form of Mexican beer drinking) is caused by the sun spewing billions of tons of magnetized plasma barf out into space. And if the billions of tons of cosmic projectile-vomiting happen to be aimed at mother earth, let's just say things could get "messy."

It pains me to say this: This is NOT a joke. This is REAL, people! I read it in the USA TODAY—but not TODAY—yesterday. I was in the USA though. So, just to be clear; I read the story about the space storm in the USA TODAY, IN the USA, YESTERDAY.

And in an AMAZING coincidence, I also read about this in a UK publication called (and I'm NOT joking) "The Sun." Here's an actual quote from "The Sun" about this space storm from the sun (I mean from the REAL sun—the star—not the publication [although there DOES happen to be another publication called "The Star"]). So, here's what "The Sun" (the publication) had to say:

"Chillingly, experts would only know about the cataclysmic phenomenon 15 minutes before it ploughs into us."

Bahahaha! "The Sun" used the word "CHILLINGLY" to talk about this scorchingly hot, thermonuclear, radioactive fire-storm from the sun!

In a final CHILLING statement, OFFICIAL SPACE SCIENTIST PEOPLE warn us that, should a space storm occur; BILLIONS of tons of solar matter could come lunging at us at more than seven-MILLION-miles-per-hour!

So, I say wear a hat.

In a related announcement:

December 16, 2018, at Olympia Stadium: Coronal Mass Injection will be wrapping up their four-month national Sun Spot Tour with this final sizzling-hot Detroit event.

(Hats are strongly recommended.)

STUPID PET TRICKS

Last night, my cat did A THING I've NEVER seen her do before. Never.

There I was—sitting on the living room floor, watching TV. And my cat just sort of sauntered in and lied down on the carpet next to me.

(No. THAT'S not THE THING I'm talking about. She's done THAT before).

So, she rolled around a few times. And kind of scratched herself and stuff. And then she did this THING that I thought was kind of weird-yet-AMAZING.

There she was, lying on her stomach. And she took all four of her paws and kind of bent them up in the air simultaneously. So it was kind of like she bent them in a way they don't normally bend. So, if you can picture this, she was lying on her stomach, but all four paws were up in the air—ABOVE HER HEAD. Like she was some sort of feline prisoner of war. And she did this with her tail too—which WASN'T so odd because her tail normally DOES bend that way. And then she kind of waggled her paws (and tail) ever so slightly—sort of FLUTTERED them—so it almost looked like they were flapping above her head. And then she picked her head up so her chin was off the carpet and she kind of squinted her eyes.

And as she did this, it made her look like she was SKYDIVING right there on the living room floor! Like she was free falling, plummeting toward the earth, paws (and tail) being blown above her head, right there on the carpet…

Oh, wait…

I don't have a cat…

Damn vodka.

SOOPERPOWERS

The farce is strong with this one.

SIGN LINGO

If it's bad manners to talk with your mouth full, would it be rude for the hearing impaired to sign while holding a sandwich?

How about a chicken leg? *

*Trick question. Chicken legs can't sign.

SMART AI

Many people think that we are NOT in danger of being surpassed by AI (Artificial Intelligence)—that computers will never be smarter than us. But I believe I have already seen evidence of this happening. For instance, how many times have you found yourself in a conversation with someone who keeps fiddling around with their smartness phone and thinking to yourself:

"Ya. The phone's probably smarter."

SPIRIT ANIMAL

As many of you know, I've been a practicing martial artist for more than two decades. At one point, a few years ago, my sensei took me aside and explained the concept of a spirit animal to me. He explained to me that one's spirit animal is not assigned, it is revealed. It is not given, earned nor bestowed. It is innate and intrinsic to our very being. It shows itself within our movements, our attitude and our choice of techniques. And if we are to develop as a martial artist to our full potential, we must act in harmony and accordance with our spirit animal. And with that, he shared his observations with me—which, if I was to be perfectly honest, left me with a few mixed feelings…

As it turns out, my spirit animal (which at first glance doesn't seem too intimidating) is the Marshmallow Peeps chick.

On the bright side, I've been told that simple carbohydrates can be bad for you—and can be VERY dangerous to your health—and over a period of time might even KILL you…

So…

There's that.

SEAL OF APPROVAL

Chevrolet has an option that when you order a new Corvette, they will give you the actual time and date when your actual Corvette is actually being built and you can actually drive down to Bowling Green, Kentucky and actually see your ACTUAL car being actually built. And I think this is actually a REALLY cool option because it actually reminds me of Taco Bell.

When I go into a Taco Bell and order a burrito; I can literally stand back behind the front of the counter and watch the people in the back (who are positioned up front so you can watch them) make my burrito.

They pull a big old tortilla off the shelf and smooth it out nice and flat before carefully building the entire inside of the burrito by squirting a series of foodstuffs onto the big, flat tortilla from a variety of giant, plastic squeeze bottles. When the squirting is over, they fold the sides of the tortilla, fold the bottom, roll it up a little and fold that top flap over. And as I watched the whole operation, it occurred to me that the tortilla is EXACTLY like an envelope—but WITHOUT the glue. It's as if you wrote a letter, then squirted it into an envelope, but then DIDN'T SEAL IT!

See? THAT'S the problem—not sealing the burrito.

I mean, what holds that top flap IN PLACE??? Friction? Capillary action? Burrito elves? Some kind of tortilla micro-gravity? Nothing very reliable I'm guessing.

So, I've worked out a solution in case I ever work at Taco Bell. Whenever I made a Burrito, I would carefully and neatly lick the flap before sealing it up to make sure it was a nice, high-quality food item before I allowed it to be passed off to the customer. Now… before you say it, I know EXACTLY what you're going to say:

Smart! Good thimking.

And I thank you for your compliment—even if you just thought it and didn't actually say it out loud. But what you probably DIDN'T think of is, there's also a small problem with my process—a problem with germs—tooth germs. But, once again, as you probably guessed; I'm on it.

Hire toothless people to build burritos. I'll bet there are PLENTY of toothless people who would just LOVE to work for Taco Bell. And Taco Bell could probably get some sort of government funding because there's probably some kind of federal program for "helping the toothless." But here's the point: NO TEETH EQUALS NO TEETH GERMS! Problem solved. In fact, I hypothesize if we could have toothless people lick ALL of our food; we could totally eradicate ALL germs the world over!

Of course, with the popularity of Taco Bell—all those people "Running for the Border"—there might not be enough toothless people to go around. So, in order to meet demand, Taco Bell could A) pull out more people's teeth, or B) put up signs:

Employees Must Brush Teeth (If You Got Any) Before Returning to Work

They could hang them in all their public restrooms—right next to the "Employees must wash hands…" sign.

Because we all know THAT sign works pretty well.

SPINNER, SCHMINNER

I don't really "get" the Fidget Spinner. Spinning that goofy little thing just doesn't look like fun—CERTAINLY not as much fun as… say…

Sitting down for an evening with a bottle of rum and a John Wick movie. And…

Taking a drink every time John snuffs out someone's wick.

SON BURN

"SPF 40,000? I'm not entirely sure that'll be GOOD enough…

"And don't forget to WEAR A HAT!!!"

—ICARUS'S MOM

SO?

"They" say, that once old people reach a "certain age", they don't care about anything anymore.

I say, so what? And why do "they" keep BOTHERING me with this nonsense?

SOFA BED SURVIVAL

Flipping through a book called THE COMPLETE WORST-CASE

SCENARIO SURVIVAL HANDBOOK, I was DRAWN to a short chapter called HOW TO ESCAPE FROM A COLLAPSED SOFA BED—because I've had SO many near-death experiences with sofa beds over the course of my lifetime.

So, they had this whole big, multi-step escape procedure. They tell you to do things like "grasp the edge" and "get your arms free" and "wriggle" and "push with your heel" and "grab a sofa arm." And there was this whole confusing THING that you had to do involving both arms, one leg, a spatula, an extraordinarily large quantity of spit, a scissors jack, and a stout woman's brazier.

And as I read the complex instructions, I realized it was just EXACTLY as I had thought:

You simply CAN'T escape from a collapsed sofa bed.

CHAPTER NINETEEN
Talent, Typpos, and the TSA

TSA: TEST OF SKILL AND AGILITY

So, here's what's hard about flying:

EVERYTHING.

You drive to the airport and as soon as you are on the property, you are faced with a deluge of information and an overwhelming number of decisions. Do I want arrivals or departures? Domestic? International? Delta? Lufthansa? NASA? Then there are signs for the rental car return, long-term parking, short-term parking, blue lot, green lot, Sir Mix-a-Lot. You're surrounded by buses, shuttles, taxis. Do I drive to the upper level? Lower level? Why are the AIRPORT POLICE waving and yelling at MY car?

Finally, you get into the parking garage. You drive to the UPPER DECK. You walk DOWNSTAIRS. You ride the elevator UPSTAIRS. Walk ACROSS to the terminal on the PEDESTRIAN BRIDGE. You take the escalator DOWNSTAIRS. You ride the SHUTTLE to the OTHER TERMINAL. And you finally get to your TICKET COUNTER.

But things are different than they used to be. It used to be, you just walked up to the ticket counter and handed the lady your ticket. Then she went klackety-klackety-klackety-klack-KLACK on her typewriter-computer thingy for 15 minutes and then tied a luggage tag on your bag and sent you off to your gate.

Now you have to go to the KIOSK. And through the miracle of electronic touch screens, YOU suddenly get to be an airline ticket agent. You enter your flight number, passport number, credit card number, frequent flier number, seat number, number of passengers, date of birth, date of departure, date of arrival, and your Aunt Wilma's custom-foot-orthotics serial number.

Then the machine spits out a luggage tag and YOU have to figure out how to attach it to your luggage. You squint at your little tag and there are lines, arrows, diagrams, and instructions—and little dotted "loopy" things printed on the tag in a 4-point-font size. And here's the tricky part: CERTAIN parts of the tag come apart to expose a sticky patch of glue and certain OTHER parts of the tag ALSO come apart to expose a sticky patch of glue—but aren't SUPPOSED to. And if you get it wrong, a TSA agent will set your bag on fire and then make you take your shoes off while he watches it burn.

So, you're done with the kiosk and it's time to get back in line to go visit the actual human ticket agent. You show her your boarding pass, driver's license, passport, credit card, frequent flier card, itinerary, AARP card, birth certificate, and Captain Midnight Secret Decoder Ring. And after YOU have just spent the last half hour poking at the kiosk touch screen like a ravenous pigeon pecking away at a tasty bug dinner, you would think SHE doesn't have to klackety-klackety-klackety-klack-KLACK on her typewriter-computer thingy for 15 minutes. But she DOES.

Then she inspects your luggage tag to make that all is in order—that you've read the illegible instructions correctly and you haven't glued your foot to your tag or anything. And if all is well, she scowls at you and dumps your bag onto a conveyor, like some disgruntled felon mandated to do community service might heave road kill into the back of a pickup truck. And for a short moment you feel PROUD—as proud as if your mom had just hung your latest artwork up on the refrigerator (which, by the way, looks less like a cat and more like a startled Jell-O globule with legs and a staph infection). The scowling ticket agent looks down at you over the top of her glasses, points, and sends you off to TSA.

At one point in time, the TSA inspection may have been a security measure, but I doubt it. Whatever the original motive, today it is both a test of skill and agility for the airline passenger and a source of endless entertainment for the TSA agents.

The contestant is asked to remove laptops, cameras, electronic devices, liquids, small children, etc. from bags, purses, backpacks and other luggage and place them into a little train of restaurant bus pans placed on a moving conveyor. Simultaneously, the contestant must unzip, unbutton and remove all coats, jackets, hats and other outerwear while removing their footwear and hopping on one foot to keep pace with their little railroad train of bus pans. While flailing, hopping along and flinging all their belongings into the TSA Zephyr (which is what I like to call my little bus pan railway) the contestant is also asked to remove their belt, cell phone and left collarbone also to be frantically hurled into the Zephyr.

The contestant is then herded down the cattle chute into a giant MRI machine where they are asked to do the chicken dance while being whirled around with their hands above their head (STILL, I might add, without a belt). Meanwhile, in a restricted clandestine facility somewhere in Kansas, other TSA agents sit in rows of comfy movie theater seats and review your MRI "results" on giant wall-mounted TV screens and remark to each other just how humorous the world would be if everyone flew naked.

Procedural Note: If at any time during the process, the contestant is found to be in possession of any sort of FINGERNAIL CLIPPERS, they will be tased, waterboarded and sent to the beginning of the line to begin anew.

Upon receiving your TSA GLADIATOR AWARD, you are free to proceed to your gate.

Gathering your possessions, you go DOWN the hall, UP the escalator and board the TRAM to the OTHER TERMINAL. Then DOWN the stairs, THROUGH the food court, UP the other stairs, ACROSS the moving walkway, DOWN the hall, ACROSS two more moving walkways and finally (after a quick visit to the restroom) … to your gate.

After a 45-minute wait, all that's left to do is figure out WHEN to get on the airplane. Listening to the garbled announcements, you have one last decision to make. Are you in Zone 1? Group 2? Preboarding? Sky Pilot Perks? First Class? Second fiddle? Steerage?

JUST TELL ME WHEN TO GET ON!!!

So, you've FINALLY made it to your seat. You've had to negotiate the on-airport driving and parking maze. You've managed to negotiate the check-in and boarding pass process. You've made it through the TSA CHALLENGE-OF-HUMILITY. You've managed to find your gate and board the airplane. You are tired, but you are proud. It has not been easy getting to this point. You feel like SPECIAL FORCES TRAINING would have been easier than this. You realize that you are sitting here only because you have utilized your impressive SKILL SET of intelligence, knowledge, creativity, ingenuity, and flexibility.

Then you look up and… with great fanfare and seriousness… using demonstrations, props, and the on-board public address system; the flight crew…

Shows you how to work a seatbelt.

THE QUEEN OF DRYLAND

We have once AGAIN come to an educational portion of this book:

BOB MATTHEWS'S HISTORICAL HISTORY OF PAST AND FORMER HISTORICAL EVENTS

The Queen of Dryland

So, way back around a-hundred-and-fifty years ago in 1880, the queen of Thailand (who had a VERY long name so I'm leaving it out of this thing) was riding on a boat with her one-year-old daughter. She was riding on this boat for a very good reason. She was unable to swim and had to go somewhere that involved water. Her one-year-old daughter ALSO couldn't swim and ALSO had to go somewhere that involved water. And… to boot (whatever THAT means) she was ALSO pregnant (the queen with the VERY long name—NOT the one-year-old daughter).

This lack of swimming ability on both party's parts was suddenly and dramatically demonstrated a little bit later during the boat ride—when the boat annoyingly flipped over and sank.

The extensive research I did for this little write-up, revealed that there were many "onlookers" (whatever THAT means) present at the royal dunking. And as the queen with the VERY long name and her daughter floundered for their lives in deep water (did I mention that neither of them could swim?); the many "onlookers" (whatever THAT means) responded rapidly and decisively in a daring, coordinated attempt to save the lives of the drowning royal females.

They threw coconuts at them.

That's right. The extensive research I did for this little write-up, revealed that the "onlookers" (whatever THAT means) launched a volley of coconuts at the queen and her daughter. Apparently, the idea was that the coconuts were buoyant and could possibly be used by the queen with the VERY long name and her one-year-old daughter as tiny, hairy, hard-to-clutch, personal flotation devices because, I guess, royal families are famously adept at fruit-surfing. As heroic and well-thought-out as these bold rescue attempts may seem to the uninformed reader, the extensive research I did for this little write-up, was sad to report that the noble non-swimmers both drowned. So there you have it.

Oh! One more thing I feel I should mention: at the time, touching the queen in any form was "frowned upon." And by "frowned upon", I mean "punishable by death." Kind of like how touching the referee is "frowned upon" by the NFL. And by "frowned upon", I mean players could be HARSHLY EJECTED FROM THE GAME! So… kind of the same thing.

I think it's ironic that there was an official decree in effect at the time that designated any touching of the queen (including, for instance, the Heimlich maneuver or the lifeguard carry) to be a capital offense. This law was designed to PROTECT the queen and to ENSURE HER SAFETY. However (and here's the irony of the situation): this was the EXACT SAME LAW that made it okay for "onlookers" (whatever THAT means) to casually lob a volley of COCONUTS AT THEIR DROWNING QUEEN!

In summary. I would just like to summarize with a little thing I like to call "the moral of the story" which is:

I guess RANK HAS ITS PRIVILEGES.

(Note to reader: All of the facts presented above are completely factual.)

TIME DAMAGEMENT

People often ask me what I do with all that extra time now that I'm retired.

I tell them I spend about four hours a day making Amish women's bonnet replicas out of loose dog hair and empty toilet paper rolls.

The rest of my days are just wasted on stupid stuff.

TODAY IS SECOND FATHER'S DAY!

My woman-child, Kristen Matthews, gave me a VERY generous gift card on ACTUAL (first) Father's Day. She was able to do this because she and her hubby have had a significant, transient boost in their personal household micro-economy due to the spoils of their recent wedding for which I had to take out a second mortgage on my wife, Nancy Matthews, to pay for.

For HIS gift, my man-child, Alex Matthews, has chosen to make me go golfing with him today.

Yes, I know. I seem ungrateful. Many of you fathers would LOVE to go golfing today with your sons. But hear me out: To say that I am "bad" at golf is tantamount to saying the Game-O-Thrones Red Wedding may have gotten a little "out-of-hand." (As a side note, I think "Game-O-Thrones" would be a great new Lifesavers flavor). I have seen videos of me golfing and I think it would be fair to say that I look very much like a panicked old woman trying to fight off a swarm of bees with a banjo.

And to say that my son, Alex is a better golfer than I would be like saying Mother Theresa was a little "nicer" person than Joseph Stalin. The fact is, I have some basic issues: A) the ball tends to be totally uncooperative, B) those funny golf-stick-thingys also tend to be totally uncooperative, C) I'm still confused by the concept of "off-sides."

So... Alex checked the weather and said it was going to be "cloudy with a chance of beating the pants off of dad" later in the day.

There. That's my day. (And I managed to mention everyone in my immediate family in that post) ... (except our dog, King Cosmo).

(There it was.)

TODAY, SECOND FATHER'S DAY IS OVER

So. Second Father's Day is over. Final score for 18 holes:

Alex 103, Dad 160…

CLEARLY making ME the winner!

TIME TRAVAILS

If I could invent a time machine, go back in time, pick up Thomas Jefferson, and transport him forward to today—you know—just to show him around…

I feel like he'd have a difficult time getting the hang of the Garden Weasel.

TAINTED SALAMANDER

I feel like TAINTED SALAMANDER would be a REALLY good name for a band.

THE 2017 SOLAR ECLIPSE

The 2017 solar eclipse was pretty much a major disappointment for me. At the point of the TOTAL eclipse (actually, I'm in the 79% zone so technically I should say at the point of the TOTAL PARTIAL eclipse) a big CLOUD rolled on by and ironically ECLIPSED the whole event. But, I've already formulated a plan for next time.

Next time I'm planning on flying to the sun. In this way, I will be staring back at the earth, which thankfully, is NOT a raging fireball (now THAT would be global warming). Then, I can watch the moon blot out the earth (at least the Marshall Islands) and I won't have to be concerned about CLOUDS. And THINK of the money I'll save because I won't need those special NASA-approved paper sunglasses. Because rumor-has-it you're NOT supposed to stare directly into the sun. So, if like me, you never bought any special NASA-approved paper sunglasses or you were one of those poor Sols (get it?) who inadvertently bought some of those unsafe, counterfeit, NASSAU-approved sight-canceling eyeglasses; you'd have to stay ALERT, CONCENTRATE, and continually fight your natural urge to look directly at the sun.

Because this is one time in life if you lose your focus, you WILL lose your focus.

THE FACEBOOK MANUAL

So—Mark Zuckerberg sent me a copy of THE Facebook Manual this morning—you know, the definitive guide on how we should conduct ourselves on Facebook.

I didn't know this, but apparently, it is a strict requirement that we ELITE FACEBOOK HUMANS post photos of everything we eat. And THE MANUAL assures me that this is strictly for the BENEFIT of all my Facebook friends. Because APPARENTLY all of my Facebook friends are interested (dare I say OBSESSED) with the tiniest of mundane details of my captivating routine daily life—including my own personal daily meal plan and whether or not I have pooped today. (Not yet.)

THE MANUAL also informed me (and I did NOT know this) that I am EQUALLY interested (dare I say OBSESSED) with the tiniest of mundane details of all my Facebook friends' captivating routine daily lives. So please let me know in the comments below if YOU'VE pooped yet today. (No photos please.)

THE MANUAL further assures me that I should post candid photos of my captivating routine daily life (such as me clipping my toenails or drinking special, limited-edition Red Bull straight out of the special, limited-edition Red Bull can) NOT because I am an insecure, narcissistic, self-absorbed little man who believes that the world revolves around the details of my ordinary, middle-class, white-bread, undistinguished life—but because this is ALL interesting, breaking news concerning my compelling, hyper-fascinating life and my friends DEMAND to stay unceasingly informed.

Well, yesterday was Nancy's birthday. We both had pasta. I'd include a photo but my smartness phone kept giving me nothing but endless pictures of my own eyeball.

Dumb smartness phone.

Think I'll go make an unboxing video now.

TRAPPED

I just spent nine hours today in a car ALONE with my wife. Nine hours with NO ONE BUT HER.

And ALL DAY for NINE HOURS, it was nothing but nonstop yack, yack, yack. Blab, blab, blab. Nothing of ANY import. Nothing at all. NOT A THING.

Just NINE HOURS of nonstop yapping, babbling, ranting, spouting, chattering, jabbering, gabbing, yammering, prattling, dare I say blathering away?

After several hours, it just simply GOT TO BE TOO MUCH.

"JUST DRIVE!" she yelled. "SHUT UP AND DRIVE!

"AND WHAT DID I TELL YOU ABOUT SINGING WITH THE RADIO??!!!"

TALK ABOUT SWEAT SOCKS!

We have all kinds of chemical products that we smear all over our bodies to mask the fact that we're sweating or even to KEEP us from sweating.

We have deodorants, antiperspirants, foot powders, sprays, roll-ons, rub-ons, and squirties. But, here's the thing: I think we should feel very FORTUNATE that we are able to sweat. Dogs, for instance, don't sweat. To cool their bodies, they have to pant to get rid of excess body heat, which frankly, looks pretty undignified.

Ostriches have a peculiar (and, in my humbug opinion, even MORE undignified) temperature regulation strategy—similar to sweating but without those pesky sweat glands ("sans glands" if you will). They urinate on their legs. That's right. Ostriches PEE ON THEIR LEGS to cool off. Then the liquid evaporates, just like our sweat does, and cools them off.

And you thought YOU had a foot odor problem.

THE POWER OF VISUALIZATION

My wife Nancy Matthews and I have been on probably a dozen cruises over the past five or six years. The atmosphere on cruises, as you might suppose, is always laid-back and relaxed. Lots of sun, food, and free time—not to mention the Caribbean ambiance. So, in my mind, free time translates to OPPORTUNITY. So, I'd like to offer this little tip for making times like this a little more productive if you'd wish to. In my case, I wanted to use the spare time to practice and improve my Sanchin-Ryu karate. But you can do anything with it. This technique is an "all-purpose" technique. It will work in almost ANY area of your life.

Before I leave home—before each and every cruise, I VISUALIZE going up to the sports deck in the morning and practicing my Sanchin-Ryu karate. I don't just WISH to do my Sanchin-Ryu, or THINK ABOUT doing my Sanchin-Ryu. I VISUALIZE doing my Sanchin-Ryu. I actually EXPERIENCE the brightness and warmth of the sunshine, the gentle rock of the ship under my kata-performing feet, and hear the hissing and splashing of the Caribbean as our vessel plows its way through it.

And sure enough (having created the proper mindset), on EVERY SINGLE DAY of the cruise, WITHOUT FAIL, I would faithfully rise in the mornings, faithfully go up to the sports deck, and faithfully VISUALIZE doing my Sanchin-Ryu at home (while lying in the sun).

Feel free to pass this tip along if it works for you.

THINGS

Always remember:

All things that ARE "a thing", started out as things that WEREN'T "a thing."

TUNDRA TEMPERANCE

Apparently (and I am NOT making this part up) it is illegal in Alaska to serve alcoholic beverages to a moose.

Really. Here's why (I think):

If you give a moose a muffin, he'll want some beer to go with it.
So you'll bring out some of your hubby's homemade Kodiak Bear Brewski.
When he's finished drinking the yummy home-brewed sudsy beverage,
He'll want another. And another. And another.
When they're all gone,
He'll throw up in your bathtub and pass out in your bed...
With one hoof on the floor to avoid Bear Brewski bed spins.

So that's why it is illegal in Alaska to serve alcoholic beverages to a moose. I'm not sure what the ruling is on medical marijuana.

(Apologies to Laura Numeroff)

TODAY'S CRYPTIC REFERENCES POST

I'm just a Jeepster for your love.

What does that EVEN MEAN? I think perhaps T. Rex has ingested too many toilet lawyers.

TOILET SWIRLS

Today, I had to go to the bathroom (number one). But before I went, I decided to try something new. I decided to spin around nine times in the bathroom—right there in front of our toilet. It went okay for the first few rotations, but by the time I had completed my fifth spin, I was starting to get REALLY dizzy. And by spin number seven, my legs unexpectedly gave out and I fell down and clipped the front of the toilet with the forehead part of my cranium. Boy did that hurt!

I just don't understand HOW my dog does it.

TREEGEDY

What if you had a best friend—someone who had lived right next door to you for DECADES. And one day, "they" came and took him away—just uprooted him, threw him in a truck and carted him off.

And later, you found out that there was a process where they took his now-lifeless body and made it into a roll of very fine paper. And later you found that trees used this very fine paper—made from the remains of your best friend—to WIPE THEIR BUTTS.

How would YOU like it?

TALENT

I know I make it look easy.

But believe me, it takes a fair amount of hard work and sophistication to be THIS dumb on a daily basis.

(Without going into politics.)

TRANSPARENT GUMMINT?

I don't get it! What's all this crazy goin's on about government transparency? I say we don't need no TRANSPARENT government!!!

We want those guys so's we can see em REAL GOOD—and keep an EYE on them!

THE REALITY OF WEIGHT LOSS

There are so many different weight-loss diets, systems, and products on the market nowadays. With all of these approaches, how do we know what really works? There seems to be no clear way for us, the average consumer, to evaluate their effectiveness. So, I've come up with a new and fresh idea that would solve this problem for us.

Reality TV shows seem to be the big fad nowadays. We have dozens of reality shows to choose from but unfortunately, most of them are total wastes of our time. Isn't it about time that we had a reality show that was useful and informative? I think it would be great to have a reality TV show that pitted diet products against each other—head to head. Here's how it would work:

Each team would be given a rhinoceros. Using their preferred weight-loss system, the first team to turn it into a unicorn wins.

THE WRECKONING

I AM A FARCE TO BE RECKONED WITH!

I reckon.

TIMELY CHOICES

In our every waking minute, we CHOOSE how we experience the world—how we represent it to ourselves. All things, objects, events, communications come to us through our senses—through our REPRESENTATIONAL SYSTEMS—through our eyes, through our ears, through our sense of touch. However, we make a CHOICE on how we interpret each piece of information that comes to us from our environment. Are we more biased toward what we see? Or do we give more weight to what we hear? Or, perhaps, the things we smell? Is it "good"? Is it "bad"? Is it "a threat"? This is true of everything we experience as we navigate through life—even in the tiniest of daily, detailed, mundane acts.

For instance, when we look at a clock. How do we interpret what we see? We DO have a choice:

Is it "2:42"? Is it "14:42"? Or is it "eighteen minutes to three in the afternoon"?

NO! IT'S 9:30 IN THE MORNING!

You're an idiot!

(Sometimes I don't even know why I bother trying.)

THUNDER THEFT

If you actually DID steal someone's thunder, where would you put it?

And you just KNOW they're gonna want it back. So how could you POSSIBLY hide anything that noisy?

PEOPLE! Where's your PLAN??? Exactly WHAT is going on inside of your head-melons???

Am I the ONLY ONE THIMKING here???

TOO HOT TO HANDEL

"Yes, music IS my life. But sometimes… and, I don't know what it IS… but it feels like I'm in the Groundhog Day song… like life is one big DEJA VU… as if the record is skipping."

-AL CODA

TURNING 65

Well, today's my birthday. I'm turning 65 today. 65! I think this is the OFFICIAL old-people's transition age. This is the age where people officially begin worrying and whispering to each other that you might suddenly die.

And that is actually the meaning of the Happy Birthday greeting: "Congratulations on not dying." That's what it means.

Here's how it works. Each year on your birthday, people say or write "Happy Birthday" to you. And you take that to mean something pleasant like, "Have a nice time on your birthday" or "Have fun today" or something like that. But what they're really thinking is more pragmatic. "Hmmm. Another year, not dead. Thought he'd be dead by now. Oh well—soon, I'm sure. Soon." And this goes on every year you're alive.

But just try and die one year, and SUDDENLY, on your birthday—NOTHING. Nadda. Bupkis. No greetings. No "Happy Birthday." No presents. No parties. No celebrations. Nothing. It's like you fell off the face of the earth (foreshadowing). Because IT MAKES NO SENSE to say "Congratulations on not dying" TO A DEAD PERSON!

And I guess that's okay. That's the way it should be. No congratulations are in order—really. Birthday presents are just adult versions of the participation trophy. All I did to reach my 65th birthday was to ride the earth around the sun 65 times. That's it. That's what we're celebrating. For 65 trips, I managed to stay on. I didn't slide off the earth and drift off into space.

But I AM grateful. I have a great life, great family, great friends and a body that basically "still works." I'm happy. And just to be clear:

I may not have done much to earn it, but I'm not OPPOSED to the adult participation trophy.

TIME FOR A CHANGE

People have been telling me that they're annoyed with this whole task of switching their clocks twice a year in order to accommodate daylight savings time. I guess we're ALL tired of springing forward and falling down in order to keep in sync with everyone else—except for me. Personally, I don't mind so much. Once I figured out how to program my DVR, adjusting clocks and watches seems so easy. (Author's Note: The previous statement was largely just wishful thinking. I still haven't figured out how to program my DVR. In fact, I'm not sure my cable service even GAVE me a DVR. I'm not even sure I have CABLE. I DO have a TV. [But I keep missing all my shows because my watch is an hour off.]) But I digress.

Nowadays; many clocks, watches, phones, computers, wives, etc. adjust the time automatically for you. Every year they string forward and fall over totally without human interdiction. So that's good. That takes care of part of the problem.

So, in my new plan (did I mention I had a new plan?), I think the government should mandate that ALL clocks should adjust themselves automatically. In the event that you have an older clock that does not adjust itself—like an old grandfather clock or a sundial or a town-crier, the government would send a robot around to each house that would run around your house adjusting all the clocks. (Did you get that I just suggested that the government "grandfather in" grandfather clocks?)

In the unlikely event that the government would be unwilling to appropriate the necessary funds to send time-setting robots around to each and every house, I'm certain that the Jehovah's Witness organization would be happy to provide this service. (Be prepared to do some "light" reading.)

In addition to resetting all your clocks, if you just happened to have a drawer containing 12-15 or so digital watches with dead batteries, the time-setting robots would also install new batteries in each of the watches before resetting the time. (I'm adding this feature for a friend.)

But here's the REAL beauty of my plan. This wouldn't just happen twice a year. This would happen EVERY SINGLE DAY. That's right—EVERY day. Every day, your clocks would all fall over backward one hour. Then we would have an extra hour each day! 25-hour days. Let me say that again. 25 HOUR DAYS! If you think we're saving time now, just THINK of the time we would save with my new plan. It would be like daylight savings time on SPHEROIDS! It would be like daylight savings time with a big shot of TOSTESTERONE! It would be as if daylight savings time had GONE POSTAL! Think of it! If Archimedes was alive today, my plan would once again have him running joyfully naked through the center of Syracuse yelling, "URETHRA"!!!

And as long as the time-setting robots were going to be there every day…

We might as well have them vacuum the floors.

THIS IS SPINAL TOAST

I blame EVERYTHING on my wife—whether it's actually her fault, or not. I know this about myself and so does she. I'm totally fine with it. It annoys the CRAP out of her.

ME: THIS TOAST IS BURNT! WHY CAN'T I GET A DECENT PIECE OF TOAST IN THIS HOUSE!!! I HATE BURNT TOAST!!!

THE WIFE: SHUT UP!!! I TOLD you not to turn the toaster ALL THE WAY UP!!!

[pause]

ME: But this one goes to 11.

THE BIG SLEEP

How come when people fall into a coma…

They don't call it "Awake Deprivation"?

TOO MUCH STATIC

While pumping gas for my car today, I noticed a sign warning me about static electricity fire danger. So now I've got a big problem:

How am I EVER going to refuel my gas-powered Van de Graaff generator?!!!

"THE NASHVILLE"

Whenever I write about Nancy and I driving to Nashville, I always like to write it like this: "the Nashville"—preceded by a "the" and within quotation marks. So here's an example of how I might use this construction in a sentence:

Nancy and I went to "the Nashville."

I realize that some other people would simply just write "Nashville" (but without the quotation marks), but I feel that that's JUST NOT GOOD ENOUGH. I feel that that would be confusing and ambiguous. They might be talking about ANY Nashville in the world. But… when I write,

Nancy and I went to "the Nashville",

people AUTOMATICALLY know that Nancy and I went to THE Nashville—the one that they're thinking of—not some other, lesser Nashville. But if I were to simply just write:

Nancy and I went to Nashville,

people would NOT be certain that we went to THE ACTUAL

Nashville—the one that they're thinking of. And that maybe we went to some other, INFERIOR Nashville that they HADN'T thought of—like some Nashville that might be a suburb of Woonsocket, Rhode Island or one that might be three-miles just outside of Zortman, Montana. Or one that might be in some kinda totally FOREIGN COUNTRY—like Hawaii, or Europe, or Cleveland.

And if some unlikely day came that Nancy and I went to a different Nashville like the Europe Nashville or the Woonsocket Nashville, I would write it like this (notice there are NO quotation marks.):

Nancy and I went to the other Nashville.

I just feel that this all just makes things so much more less not clear.

THE MIDEAST

I read that people in that Middle East have been fighting with each other for MORE THAN A BILLION YEARS! And that seems like a long time to me. Over the centuries, various powers have tried to intervene and solve the mystery of unrest in the Middle East—yet NONE have been successful. But I have my own theories.

I live in Michigan. And, here in Michigan; when winter is upon us, and the skies are gray, and the snowfall covers the landscape and makes everything look flat and featureless; many people get SAD. Not "sad" as in, "I feel really sad since Honey Boo Boo went off the air." Or, "My wife was out horseback riding and an airplane landed on her and squished her. I feel really sad—I sure LOVED that horse."

I mean SAD, as in Seasonal Affective Disorder—when people get crabby-sad (NOT crab-salady) crabby-sad—because they're imprisoned, for months at a time, in the emotionally depressing Michigan winter doldrums.

But when spring comes and the sun shines and the grass comes up, the SADness disappears. Everyone's disposition improves. Life becomes FUN again. But THAT'S the Midwest—and I didn't come here to talk about the MidWEST. I came here to talk about the Middle EAST.

My theory is that people in the Middle East have remained cranky enough to continue battling each other for MORE THAN A BILLION YEARS because they too are afflicted with SAD—SAND Affective Disorder. Similar to SEASONAL Affective Disorder—but with sand.

Now, I've never actually BEEN to the Middle East, but I've seen pictures. I've also seen sand—and those two things look alike to me. My theory is that all that sand ubiquitously covering the Middle Eastern landscape makes everything look flat and featureless—just like the winter snows morph the scenery here in Michigan. But, just like here, a little grass and greenery could solve the problem, lighten the mood, and cheer everyone up. So, since the solution seems so OBVIOUS and EASY, that begs the question…

Say it with me…

Why can't everyone JUST GET A LAWN?!!

[rimshot]

TROMPE L'OEIL

By now, most of you have seen photos of a type of street art called trompe l'oeil (which, I think, is French for "stomp on Lowell"). It's a form of optical illusion art where, from a certain angle, two-dimensional paintings look like actual, genuine-article, bona fide three-dimensional objects. So, for instance, street artists will paint big canyons in the middle of the road and it will look like there's an actual, genuine-article, bona fide, humongous, craterous, big-honkin' canyon (complete with waterfall) eroding away your local bypass. Or they'll paint their garage door to look like an actual, genuine-article, bona fide jet fighter is parked inside (missiles aimed at YOUR house). Really fun stuff.

And now, road engineers in Iceland have found a way to have fun with this fun stuff AND get paid for it. They have painted crosswalks on the road that, from the driver's perspective (and this is the truth), look like giant, floating cement blocks. So as drivers approach the intersection, it looks as if there are massive anti-tank obstacles hovering a couple feet above the road. And that causes them to slow down. But as they get closer, they realize that these "blocks" were just optical-delusion-anti-tank obstacles that had been stomped flat like Lowell, and they simply roll through the intersection—albeit, at the desired lower speed. A similar technique is being tried out in North America (and this ALSO might be the truth), where one town has painted stomp-on-Lowell (SOL) potholes in the road to make drivers slow down for intersections.

So, if I was one of these illusionist road engineers, I think it would be fun to paint a stomp-on-Lowell "BRIDGE OUT" sign on the road to get people to slow down. And as they approached, they'd realize it was just an optical confusion and they'd keep going. So, after that, I'd paint another sign that said, "NO. REALLY! BRIDGE OUT" to get them to slow down again. And I'd follow these two with a third SOL sign: "I SAID: BRIDGE OUT! ARE YOU DEAF?!!"

And, of course, I'd place these three signs just up the road from a bridge that really WAS out—and, I know what you're thinking…

HEY! What fun!

Now, I believe that MOST people are going to realize when they get to the bridge-out-situation; that it's an actual, genuine-article, bona fide bridge-out-situation and NOT an optical contusion. But there's going to be at least that ONE GUY:

"Fool me once, shame on me. Fool me three times, I'll KICK YOUR ASS!"

And he's going to mash that accelerator to the floor and launch himself off that actual, genuine-article, bona fide broken bridge out onto a tenuous platform of largely unsupportive air molecules. His first thought will be some form of,

"Oopsie."

And then gradually, his feeling of panic will be replaced by a relieved and calm feeling of relief and calmness as he looks down and sees the large, friendly, welcoming, MAGNIFICENT safety net that I have handily placed below for his comfort and benefit.

I know… I know… You're thinking: "It's a fake! It's a fake! It's just another stomp-on-Lowell optical-pollution-thing. YOU'RE A MONSTER!"

But NO! I would NOT do that to him. I would actually put out a REAL NET—a REAL-LIFE, ACTUAL, GENUINE-ARTICLE, BONA FIDE safety net. REALLY! I would. HONEST!

I'd lay it right there on the ground.

TALKING SKELETONS

You know how everywhere you look, you see TALKING SKELETONS? Skeletons just standing there with that hinged jaw flapping away and yapping about stuff?

Well, I'm here to set you straight. THAT JUST CAN'T HAPPEN!

Theoretically speaking, anyone with even HALF-a-brainless knows that a talking skeleton couldn't move its jaw. It's impossible. BECAUSE IT HAS NO MUSCLES. It only has bones—BECAUSE IT'S A SKELETON! Bones (like the skin of a pumpkin) are there for support and structure. Muscles (like rubber bands and cherry bombs) are what do the moving. So that flapping jaw is a hoax (just like ALL of Disneyland)! So next time you see a talking skeleton, you'll KNOW that that's an IMPOSSIBLE thing going on there and that it's NOT REAL…

UNLESS it's a VENTRILOQUIST skeleton. Then RUN!!! Because it will EAT you!!!

Oh, wait…

It CAN'T CHEW.

THERE'S ALWAYS ROOM

Don't get me wrong—I LIKE Jell-O. Especially orange. Orange is my favorite—either orange or RED. I like BOTH orange AND red—but neither one as much as blue—which is my favorite. I think. Blue Jell-O is the BEST—but NOT in a Jell-O SHOT. I don't "get" the Jell-O SHOT—not AT ALL. Because, as I said, I LIKE Jell-O (especially grape) …

But CERTAINLY not enough to have it INJECTED!

And besides, I think somewhere along the way, the suspended fruit cocktail particles are going to be an issue.

TOMORROW—I PROMISE

A while back I decided to join the NPAA—the National Procrastination Association of America because…

Well, YOU know why.

Today, in the mail I received an invoice from them for my 2015 dues. At least that's what my wife tells me.

I haven't read it yet.

THE HUMAN BRAIN? TOTALLY AMAZING

The human brain is a totally AMAZING thing. Think about it:

- It's less than HALF the size of your leg… YET… it can think SO much better.
- It's structurally ALMOST IDENTICAL to cauliflower… YET… it's SO much softer.
- And it smells SO fresh!

And, if you simply MUST demonstrate the AMAZINGNESS of the human brain to yourself, just walk up to ANYONE and ask them what they were doing the day Abraham Lincoln was shot. Instant recall!

"I was at home, churning butter."
"Having drinks with General Useless S. Grant."
"I was out taunting Horace Greeley because: 'Horace'."
"Exercising. Me and the other pioneer ladies were sweatin' to the minuets."
"I was out vacuuming the cattle."

So, need I say more about just HOW amazing the brain is?

I think, almost EACH AND EVERY DAY…

My OWN brain totally RE-AMAZES me!

TYPPO

I was just composting another post. And the first line started out with:

"Since I've been posting on Facebook…"

But, I had made a typo. And instead of writing what I had intended to write, I had written:

"Since I've been POSING on Facebook…"

And as I stared at what I had written and considered the two versions—corrected and uncorrected, I came to the realization that…

Now, I really DON'T KNOW which one is the typo.

THE DEMISE OF GRANDPA

When my father died, I took my daughter Kristen aside and gently broke the news to her.

ME: Grandpa went to live on a farm where he can run around and play with all the other grandpas in the sunshine.

KRISTEN: STOP THAT! No, he didn't! DAD! For heaven's sake! I'm twenty-five years old. I UNDERSTAND DEATH! I'M A NURSE!

Sometimes daughters can be SO difficult to protect.

THE MIRACLE OF TWINS

Have you noticed how twins seem to be able to communicate with each other non-verbally—almost telepathically? And how one twin always seems to know what the other one is thinking? And how often they both finish each other's sentences?

Well, not to brag, but I can do ALL of those things.

I think I might be twins.

TAO TE THING: YIN AND YAMS

Opposites DEFINE one another—because, if one is missing—then you are left with just the other (which would no longer exist).

Beauty is all around us but would not be seen as such, if other stuff didn't look like crap.

Good in this world would not exist without bad (and also "fair to middling" and "close enough for horseshoes").

Easy DEFINES difficult (but not easily).

The long and short of it is that high and low are mostly just differing degrees of each other.

Were there not FRONTS; there would most certainly NOT be front doors, lakefront property, and backfiring.

And were there not anything, there would most certainly NOT be nothing. (Unless there WAS nothing—because "not anything" IS nothing.)

However, were there NOT waffles… there would STILL most certainly be chicken. Because: eggs.

—LOUD TZU (551—479 B.C.E. GIVE OR TAKE)

CHAPTER TWENTY
Unblinkered and Udderly Uncertain

UNCERTAINTY PRINCIPLE

I'm PRETTY CERTAIN that Werner Heisenberg probably formulated his famous uncertainty principle while trying to pick out an ice cream flavor at Baskin-Robbins.

But I'm not sure.

UDDERLY ACCOUNTABLE

I went through the drive-through bank teller today. And as it turns out…

I really AM morally bankrupt.

UNBLINKERED: 2D OR NOT 2D

When you go to the movies, they give you those cheezy, semi-disposable plastic glasses in order to make the FABRICATED, 2-D movie look like REAL, 3-D real-life.

I think a good idea would be to make cheezy, semi-disposable plastic 2-D glasses for everyday life to kind of FLATTEN EVERYTHING OUT—like a movie. I think this could come in handy.

For instance, if you were feeling especially fat one day, you could have "your friend" wear the 2-D glasses and you would appear to be one of those stand-up, cardboard-cutout movie guys you see standing around in movie lobbies. Then you could stand at a 45-degree angle to "your friend"—and you would only look HALF as fat.

And then you could talk about all the weight you'd lost on some kind of trendy kiwi fruit and cocaine diet. And, if after a while, things began to get a little "weird" because you made your friend wear cheezy, plastic 2-D glasses just to listen to you go on-and-on about fruit, cocaine, Dr. Phil, Siamese hat-dancing, and those tiny little after-dinner mints that you somehow keep getting lodged in your nose…

You could just turn TOTALLY sideways and disappear…

At least until they took off the glasses.

"Hey, Bob. Looks like you put on a little weight there."

I'D buy a pair. Wouldn't you?

CHAPTER TWENTY-ONE
Vegans, Virtue, and Virginia

VEGAN SCHMEEGAN

Many of you who know me, know that I don't eat anything that poops. Many of you who DON'T know me, don't CARE what I eat.

But that's not my issue. My problem is I need something to CALL myself. Everyone calls me a "Vegan" but I HATE that word.

First of all, it has a stupid pronunciation. The word is SUPPOSED to conjure up an image of VEGETABLES. That's its job! But the idiotic way that those vegan-founding-mother-fathers chose to enunciate their made-up, moronic moniker creates a distinct, discomforting disconnect. The "g" in "vegan" is pronounced like a hard "g"—GUH, GUH—as in "gum" and "gnu." Whereas the "g" in vegetable is pronounced like a "j" (think "jalapeno").

The basic problem is, these two words DON'T SOUND ANYTHING ALIKE. Vegan. Vegetable. They don't seem associated. Just like the two words "wagon" and "wajtibble." Do those seem related? I think not!

Secondly, not only does "Vegan" have a stupid pronunciation; it is (how can I put this?) a STUPID WORD. It sounds much less like an eating philosophy and more like the name of a planet:

"Greetings! We're from the planet Vegan. Do not harm us. We come in peas."

VIRTUOUS STICKERS

While most of us admire people who STICK TO THEIR GUNS and think of them as being VIRTUOUS...

I feel they're generally just ordinary folks who have difficulty using Super Glue.

VIRGINIA ASKS A QUESTION

Why, yes Virginia…

Those ARE fink plamingoes.

CHAPTER TWENTY-TWO
Who, Why, and What the...

WAR! GOOD GOD Y'ALL!

War is different than it used to be. It used to be back in the days of Middle Earth, huge armies would face off across a massive, expansive battlefield—lined up in wave upon wave of Orcs, dwarves, men and, of course; giant, ill-tempered, walking, marauding, death-dealing TREES. And we, the civilized peoples of the world carried this "noble" tradition forward through history up until the Second World War.

Now, all wars seem to be turning into terrorist activities. Instead of fighting large, amassed forces on the open battlefield; we are battling small enemy cells—often on our OWN SOIL.

Historically, we have been lucky and safe due to our isolated geographic situation. Except for America, all other theaters of war have been within rolling distance of the enemy. But we are buffered on both sides by massive bodies of water. Since the Civil War, no enemy has engaged us on American soil—until today (not counting the Japanese balloon-bombs and those pesky German U-boats).

My point is that our world has CHANGED. Back when I was a child, we did not worry so much that the enemy would infiltrate our society and live among us. We did not worry that terrorists would blow us up in our own football stadiums, shoot us in our sushi shops, or put anthrax in our venti-half-whole-milk-half-soy-extra-foam-salted-caramel-mochaccino-lattes. We grew up in a world free of these types of fears.

Sure. There WAS a fairly-highly-probability chance that we and the Russians would initiate the complete and total mutual nuclear destruction of our planet. But we all KNEW that if it came down to this…

We could just calmly hide under our school desks.

WORDS... SO PRICELESS

Valuable/invaluable...

Seems like a waste of a perfectly good word in there somewhere.

WHA...?

In the land of the blind…

The one-eyed Jack is King.

WE ARE IN KY!

Nancy and I were in Kentucky and we woke up and went down to eat at the hotel restaurant. I spotted a sign on the wall that said: "Welcome to KY." I asked Nancy if this is where they made the KY Jelly and could we go see the plant...

She said, "Just eat your breakfast."

WHEN HELL FREEZES

WINTERING IN HELL

Another DARN GOOD band name!

(But kind of a mediocre-at-best retirement strategy.)

WHEN PIGS FLY

I've always loved the expression:

I'LL BELIEVE IT WHEN PIGS FLY

I love it SO MUCH that if I had been a writer on the 60s sitcom GREEN ACRES, I would have written a series of episodes where that lovable pig, Arnold Ziffel, earned his pilot's license. And maybe, just maybe, they'd still be on the air.

Also, it might have helped if the cast members hadn't ALL died.

WATCH IT!

When I was little, we had analog watches that were powered by springs. And you had to wind them up every day or two or they would stop ticking.

Years passed and someone came up with the idea of a self-winding watch. There was a little pendulum inside and as you walked and swung your arm, the weight swung back and forth and wound up the spring for you. So, as long as you didn't leave the watch laying on your dresser for a couple of days, or your arm didn't fall off at the shoulder; you NO LONGER HAD TO WIND YOUR WATCH.

The next step in the timekeeping technology progression was the digital watch. It contained a battery that didn't need to be changed for SEVERAL YEARS. So, you NEVER had to wind your watch—even if your dog ate it or you were in a coma! (Or your dog ate it WHILE you were in a coma.)

Now I have a Fitbit Blaze. It has a RECHARGEABLE battery. RECHARGEABLE. That means it has to be recharged every few days or it will stop "ticking" (electronically speaking). Isn't that, functionally speaking, pretty much the same thing as winding a watch—except it

TAKES LONGER? Ya. I used to be able to wind my watch in a matter of seconds. Now it takes TWO HOURS.

It feels like Groundhog Day, all over again.

It feels like sometimes, we as a culture, are making progress backwards.

WHY IS TEXTING "A THING"?

Whoever thought texting would become "a thing"?

I mean, there was a time when we didn't have cell phones yet but we had TYPING. And NOBODY liked typing because it was slow and required too much concentration. Typing was SO odious and despised in fact, that we used to hire specialized people to do our typing for us (just like nowadays we hire specialized people to scrape the tartar off our teeth). Back in those days, we were allowed to call them "secretaries" (the typers—not the tartar-scrapers). But we don't call them that anymore because, as it turns out, "secretaries" has become a demeaning word primarily because it reminds everyone of a much-celebrated racehorse. And no woman (which "secretaries" all used to be) wants to be compared to a horse no matter HOW fast she can run. So today we call them "administrative assistants" which is a much more respectable title apparently because it doesn't bring to mind any fleet-footed land mammals.

So "back in the day" people didn't like to type, but we did like to talk. We would chat away for HOURS on the land-line phone. So, it should be OBVIOUS if you extrapolate the simplification trend, that the next logical communication rage would surely be...

Typing with your thumbs??!

Ya. What's up with THAT? Doesn't it seem like we're going backward?

I think I've figured out what the problem was.

In between the invention of land-lining and texting, we humans came up with another little tech ditty called the ANSWERING MACHINE. This was a little tape player/tape recorder that interfaced with your land-line phone. When someone called and you didn't answer, it played a pithy little tape message for them:

"Hello, this is Dan!" "And this is Darlene!" [in unison] "Sorry we can't come to the phone now. We're down in the root cellar choking a small, feisty stranger to death right now. Please leave a detailed message after the beep and we'll get back to you as soon as we're done with this annoying little chore..." BEEEEEEEP...

This beep was a signal for the caller to immediately hang up the phone.

And therein lies the problem. We HATED talking to "the machine." If our generation (the answering-machine generation) would have had a motto, that motto would have been: "I HATE talking to those things!" And our second motto would have been: "I HATE being called 'the answering-machine generation!'" So, whenever we would get "the machine" we would curse (before the beep) and IMMEDIATELY HANG UP. And, if we managed to beat the nearly-insurmountable odds and get an ACTUAL, BONA FIDE, LIVE PERSON on the other end, we would be so shocked and surprised that we would temporarily lose all of our personal English-speaking capabilities, and IMMEDIATELY HANG UP. So, our generation, the answering-machine generation, obviously had a LOT of hang-ups. So, after a decade or so of these kinds of shenanigans, we became pretty much disenchanted with talking on the phone.

So, when typing with our thumbs came along, our thoughts kinda went like this:

It's not as good as land-lining once was. But at least it's progress.

WHOSE THEY?

Did you ever stop and wonder who "THEY" are? You know. People always refer to that omniscient, nebulous information source in the sky.

As in: "THEY" say it might rain today. Or, "THEY" say if there's a nuclear war, all that will be left will be cockroaches… and maybe hipsters. Or, "THEY" are predicting a major solar flare event this Thursday which will incinerate approximately 42% of the nation… so wear a hat.

Well just so you know: I am that mysterious "THEY" everyone references. Yep. It's ME.

"They" say I'm pretty knowledgeable.

WATCH IT

Is it, "A watched pot never boils" or…

"A watched boil never pops"?

And who gets to say?

WEAPONIZED DAIRY

I don't know what it is about cheese that makes you constipated, but my GREATEST FEAR is that evil foreign scientists are hard at work somewhere in a clandestine facility at this VERY MOMENT, trying to weaponize the American cheese supply by isolating, and then INTENSIFYING this mystery constipation factor. That's right, I worry that EVEN AS I AM WRITING THIS, nefarious forces are hard at work creating...

WAIT for it...

WEAPONS OF ASS OBSTRUCTION!

TAH DAHHH!!! (Cue the trumpets!)

WHY NOT?

Here's my question:

We have special scissors, guitars, and other items for left-handed people.

We have special braille books and signage for the visually impaired.

We have special phones and special doorbells that light up so that people with hearing impairments can see them ring.

So WHY don't we have special mirrors for people with dyslexia?

WORLD DOMINATION

I think that there's no doubt in ANYBODY'S mind that during World War II; Germany was engaged in a barbarous and relentless quest for world domination. And it's a darn good thing that the allies were able to stop Hitler before he took over the entire planet. Otherwise, we could have become…

Wait for it…

The Third Reich from the sun.

[Rimshot]

WHO?

You know that guy? That guy who used to be THAT guy?

Well…

I'M that guy.

WHAT THE... WHA?

Remember when the government or the TSA or something first wanted to install those machines where you stand up in them and hold your hands up like you're being taken prisoner of war? And then the thing whirls around you and looks at you with x-ray-sunspot vision or something? But then a bunch of complainy people complained about them—that the government or TSA or something wanted to look at naked people with no clothes on and that it violated our privates or something?

And the government or TSA or something countered with an argument that went something like: "We're not planning on looking at naked people with no clothes on, we're planning on looking at IMAGES of naked people with no clothes on and rest assured that the safety of your privates is our highest concern," or something like that. And the government or TSA or something also explicitly promised not to laugh. So, the complainy people acquiesced and said okay, what could be the harm? Go on ahead with your x-ray-sunspot vision peepshow thing.

Well, what I want to know is: you know how you go through the metal detector and your belt buckle makes the thing buzz? And then the government or TSA or something tells you to take off your belt and throw it in the dishpan and try again? And then your pants fall down, right there in the crowded airport, in plain view of everyone?

Well, what I want to know is:

WHERE ARE ALL THOSE COMPLAINY PEOPLE NOW?!!

WE'RE SO SORRY, UNCLE ALFRED

They said Alfred Einstein used to do a thing called THOUGHT EXPERIMENTS. These were little exercises where he would make up made-up hypothermical situations in his head and then play them like a movie to see what happened. For instance, this is allegedly how he invented the theory of relatives. He imagined that he was riding on a train that was traveling at the speed of light and he then turned on a flashlight to see what would happen. And then whatever happened made him invent the theory of relatives.

I got tired and didn't read what old Alfred found so I just ran the thought experiment myself. And I found that at the speed of light, the flashlight just blew right out of my hand. Ever try to hold a flashlight while traveling at the speed of light? Let me tell you, that's a LOT of wind. And if you had a dog that liked to stick its head out the window to feel the wind, the wind would probably blow its entire head RIGHT OFF—and also probably its body. So, you'd be left sitting there on a train, watching a flashlight get violently ripped out of one hand and holding a disconnected dog's tail in the other. Better to take the bus, I say. And why would you EVER bring your DOG to a speed of light thought experiment??!! I have two words for you: DON'T!! There's no need… and somehow it seems a little cruel.

So, it seems like kind of a lame experiment to me. But I didn't come here to discuss old Alfred's lame and boring physics stuff, I came here to discuss REAL WORLD problems and my thought experiments to solve them.

So, in my thought experiment, I travel back in time and pick up Abraham Lincoln (and this is important) BEFORE he was shot at the movies. And also, NOT the Lincoln Memorial guy. I want the

Abraham Lincoln (and this is also important) with the big Franklin stove hat.

I'd be sure to take my time machine with the tall ceiling to accommodate Abe's stoveskin hat. And I'd bring him back here and stick him in a room. I'd make him comfortable. Maybe sit him down in front of a big screen TV. Maybe put on an ABRAHAM LINCOLN: VAMPIRE HUNTER DVD just to make him feel at home. Maybe offer him a Zima. Then I'd be off to find the Pope.

I'd have to go get him at Vatican City—which I'm not sure where it is, but in my thought experiment, it's at the North Pole—somewhere near Santa's house. And I'd tell the Pope, "Grab your tallest hat. We've got a thought experiment to do." And he'd say, "Okay, let me go and get it." And then he'd offer me some holy Zima (because that's what Popes DO in thought experiments).

So then, I'd bring the Pope back here. I'd have to drive him back in a car with a sunroof because I wouldn't want him to smash "the hat" against the roof. And we'd make good time because, with that red hat-blob sticking out of the roof, a lot of people would mistake us for a Police car in their rearview mirror. When I got him back, I'd put him in a different room than the one Lincoln's in because I'M ABSOLUTELY SURE the Pope doesn't want to see some kind of Abraham Lincoln/vampire movie. I mean, think of it. The Pope watching an Abraham Lincoln/Vampire movie? THAT would be weird.

So, I'd go get Lincoln in his big old Ben Franklin stove hat. And I'd already have the Pope in his big, old, tall, pointy Pope hat. And then I'd stand them right next to each other, looking at me. And then in MY thought experiment…

I'd have them face off in a Limbo contest.

Thought experiments. Try them sometime. ALL of us geniuses use them.

WTF?

WTF does "WTF" mean?

WHAT'S WRONG WITH ME?

I'm afraid that I was traumatized at birth because...

Let's say that, hypotheoretically, I WAS traumatized at birth. Since it occurred at birth, I would never have known anything else. Traumatized would be my NORMAL state. I certainly wouldn't FEEL traumatized because, without ever having had anything else to compare it to, I wouldn't actually KNOW what being traumatized feels like. I would feel ABSOLUTELY NORMAL because TRAUMATIZED is how I would normally feel.

And that's EXACTLY how I DO feel—ALL the time. Normal. PERFECTLY normal.

And THAT, folks, is why I think I was traumatized at birth.

WHAT'S YOURS IS MIME

What if you had a friend who was unable to speak, and so, communicated only through gestures? And suppose this friend got trapped in a transparent box and died. So, you had to go find another replacement friend. And, as luck would have it, he ALSO was unable to speak, and so, communicated only through gestures.

QUESTION: Would you tell people you had changed your mime?

ANSWER: Unlike me, you COULD… but YOU wouldn't.

I know. I know, it's enough to blow your…

Mind.

Mind! MIND! What is WRONG with you people?!!! As the inebriated clown said to the drunken ringmaster:

"Get your mime out of the gutter!"

WHAT AM I? A MUENSTER?

Many of you don't know this about me, but I'm lactose tolerant. Yep. Lactose tolerant. That means I can have ALL the lactose I want. But, here's the thing. I'm also a vegan—NO animal products—so that means I can't have ANY of the lactose I want. And that's sad…

Because it feels like I'm just WASTING my superpower.

WE NEVER DO ANY FATHER-SON STUFF ANYMORE

When I was a young boy, my father used to start out all of his thundering, threatening, booming reprimands the same way:

"I'VE GOT HALF A MIND… !!!"

Which, by the way, is a REALLY hard thing for an infantile, ditsy, witless, adolescent youth NOT to laugh at.

"I'LL TEACH YOU TO LAUGH AT ME!!!"

"Just to be clear Dad, what you're teaching me is NOT how to laugh—but how to yell. My guess is that what WANT to teach me is how to cry."

“I'LL GIVE YOU SOMETHING TO CRY ABOUT! AND WHEN I DO… DON'T COME CRYING TO ME!!!”

“Ironically Dad, I think you've just given me something ELSE to laugh about. This really isn't going well.”

“I TOLD YOU… NO… WIRE… HANGERS… EVER!!!”

WELCOME

I think going to someone's front door is one of the great ironies of living in “modern” times.

As you approach the front door, the motion sensor flood lights pop on—bathing you in a soft, warm glow—reminiscent of prison searchlights. Simultaneously, the motion sensor also triggers the ever-vigilant Roomba lawnmower, (tactically positioned on the lawn behind you—with the handy weed-wacker/intruder-wacker attachment) putting it into “high alert standby” mode. As you push the button, the RING video surveillance “doorbell” takes your picture and informs THE OCCUPANTS of your presence. Meanwhile, the lawnbot opens a secure communication channel with “central command”; notifying them that it has acquired the target and is in the process of confirming “wacker lock-on.” As you repeatedly ring the “doorbell” and wait, the video surveillance system continues to record your actions (uploading the video to their main data archive facility in Omaha, Nebraska) while THE OCCUPANTS hide out silently in the “safe room” waiting for you to go away.

And, oh ya…

There's also a WELCOME mat.

WALKIES

I'm sure some people are wondering how our dog, King Cosmo, is doing after his spleenectomy/gallbladderectomy surgery. Well, I'm happy to report that I took Cosmo for "walkies" yesterday. (I know it's silly, but that's what HE calls it.) We only walkied about a mile. But here's the thing: it took us a more than HALF AN HOUR. So, pretty slow. For you math impoverished people—that's less than two miles per hour. Now, of course we were slow—partially because Cozzie just had MAJOR surgery three weeks ago. But mostly because there were just so very, very, VERY many things to PEE ON!

And to make matters WORSE…

COSMO peed on a few things too.

CHAPTER TWENTY-THREE
Yes, Yippy-Yappy, and Yumminess

YES!!!

"your an idiot."

This was an actual comment that I read on someone else's FaceBook post. Does this mistakenly-crafted insult strike anyone else as being IRONICALLY HILARIOUS?

In my opinion, it's like the pot calling the kettle silver (because no one uses cast iron cooking vessels anymore).

YOU'RE KILLING ME

I THINK CAPITAL PUNISHMENT SHOULD BE RESERVED FOR REALLY HEINOUS CRIMES.

For lesser crimes, it's okay to just go ahead and use lower-case punishment.

[Rimshot]

YOU KNOW YOU WANT TO

I just got a brand-new camera today and boy am I THIRSTY.

Okay—I know it said NOT to. But I really WANTED to. I couldn't HELP myself. It was just too TEMPTING.

Come on. You KNOW you've ALWAYS wanted to.

Yep. I ate the descecant.

YOU'VE GOT YOUR NIRVANA!

I wonder if Buddhist monks ever mindlessly use the phrase "YOLO."

YUMMYNESS

Maybe I've seen too much Winter Olympics on TV. Because, for some reason, one of the figure skating moves sounds ABSOLUTELY DELICIOUS to me and it's making me HUNGRY!

And you might ask, "What would that delicious-sounding Olympic figure skating move be?" And I might answer, "That would be THE TRIPLE SOW-COW."

Now, I'm not sure exactly what a triple sow-cow is in YOUR world; but in Bob's WoRld, this would most certainly be some sort of land-mammal TURDUCKEN. Here would be MY recipe for the…

TRIPLE SOW-COW SURPRISE:
(DEGREE OF DIFFICULTY: 17.1)

You will need:
3 smallish sows, 1 medium size cow, 150 gallons of Mountain Dew, salt, pepper.

- Wash, debone and defeather all three sows.
- Remove the tails and marinate in Mountain Dew (the sows, not the tails). You will know the sows are ready for the next step when the carcasses float to the surface.
- Make bacon out of the first sow while grinding the second sow into pork sausage.
- Stuff the third sow with the pork sausage, wrap it in the bacon,

and shove the whole works into a cow.

- Salt and pepper to taste.
- Grease a very large cookie sheet and lightly dust with all-purpose flour.
- Place sow-cow, snout-side-up onto the cookie sheet and cover with aluminum foil.
- Bake in a medium oven for 216 hours—basting frequently.
- Before serving, test with a toothpick to ensure pork is thoroughly cooked…

So as to avoid the unintentional DEATH SPIRAL (Degree of difficulty: 0.0).

YIPPY-YAPPY

I've noticed, ("of late"), that; in my "writing"; my "tendency" is to rely "VERY" heavily on punctuation—in order to create both—proper phrasing… proper timing… and proper EMPHASIS!!! In fact, as I "examine" 'various-and-Sunday' examples of my writing… I notice that—it's 'MOSTLY' just punctuation—separated by some #%$^@ words.

But, I suppose, I "just 'might'" be #%$^@ wrong…

%&*#%$^@

CHAPTER TWENTY-FOUR
Zen, Zoology, and Zero Foresight

ZEN OF FRIENDS

Here is the VERY COOL thing about having an imaginary friend:

Those times when one of them is mean to you and keeps calling you names and won't stop. And he points out ALL the body features and character traits that he KNOWS you're self-conscious about and laughs and laughs and LAUGHS! And he WON'T STOP laughing. ALL DAY! ALL NIGHT! Laughing! Laughing! Laughing-and-pointing. Bahahaha! Bahahaha! And he WON'T stop with the name calling! ALL DAY! ALL NIGHT! Keeping you awake at night! Name-calling! Name-CALLING! SCREAMING! SCREAMING in your head! LAUGHING!!! Bahahahahahaha! HAAAAAAAA!!! And the constant DIN is ASSAULTING your VERY MENTAL CORE—to the point where you JUST want to put on ALL your Metallica albums AT THE SAME TIME, CRANK the volume, don your RADAR HAT, cover yourself in GRAPE JELLO and cat hair; and just go out and STAB SOMETHING!!! Bahahahahahahahaha! Hahaaaa!!

At times like these, you can just poke your finger into one ear and make your imaginary friend pop out the other ear.

Sometimes that's the only way I can maintain my sanity.

ZERO FORESIGHT

When they say: Hindsight is 20-20…

I often wonder if they're talking about that guy you see backing up on the expressway shoulder because he missed his exit.

ZOOLOGY OF "MUSIC"

Ever since I can remember, I've always wanted to NEVER PLAY THE BAGPIPES. Here's why:

It LOOKS exactly like you're strangling an OCTOPUS… but it SOUNDS exactly like you're strangling a CAT.

Either way…

Strangling.

(And, before you ask: Nope, I've never SMELLED the bagpipes, so I have no idea WHAT it SMELLS exactly like you're strangling.)

BACKWARD

"You shouldn't give an audience what they want. Give them what you want."
—BUDDY MORRA

Why does this book have a Backword? Because I think having a foreword is a dreary and uninteresting way to begin a book. Besides, if I had STARTED this book with that same Buddy Morra quotation, people would have most-certainly thought, "What an arrogant, self-centered ass!" And, just to be clear, I'm not denying that. I just think that it's no way to start a book. But it's an okay way to end one; because let's face it, I've ALREADY got your money.

But I've included this potentially inflammatory quotation for a reason other than to cause inflammation. These particular words mean SO much more to me than what you might first take away at face value.

I spent every day with that quotation facing me throughout the entire process of writing this book for the simple reason that it gave me inspiration and COURAGE—courage to see this thing through to the end. Because I learned LONG ago that I'M NOT FOR EVERYONE. And I've learned to accept that. I know that face-to-face, some are going to think I'm hilarious and entertaining. I also know I'm going to annoy the CRAP out of some (many) people. That's just me. And over the course of my lifetime I've come to accept that as "just the way things are" because let's face it: that's JUST THE WAY THINGS ARE.

But it's different with writing. Speaking is SO much more transient. When I SAY something stupid, I know it will be gone the next second. FOREVER. GONE. It only continues to "exist" in peoples' minds—in our fallible and unreliable memories. But when I WRITE something and put it in print, or out on the Internet, well... that's pretty much FOREVER. For all intents and purposes, we're pretty much talking

IMMORTAL STUPIDITY. So, my tendency is to want to be “safe” in print. To be “careful.” To avoid writing the “wrong” thing or the “stupid” thing. But here's the dilemma. SO MUCH of my honest humor—the type of humor that makes ME laugh—DEPENDS on me saying or writing the “preposterous” thing or the “foolish” thing or the “illogical” thing. So, when I play it “safe”, I lose myself. When I begin to censor out the things that are “too dumb”, “too silly”, “too irrational”, or might “OFFEND someone”; I end up creating SOMEONE ELSE'S body of work. And I quickly become disinterested (and disinteresting). And, more importantly—I am lost.

So, when you get offended; when you get the urge to send me that nasty letter, that chastising e-mail, or that critical text message; remember...

I probably won't bother to read it anyway.

Bob Matthews

Commerce Charter Township, MI
September 2018

THANKS

How would you like to be the one to have to proofread this book? Think about it. This book is almost, BY DEFINITION, a total book of errors. Spelling errors, grammatical errors, punctuation errors, syntax errors—and don't EVEN get me started about the obtuse logic and extensive number of nonfactual "facts." All this makes it difficult to tell the unintentional CRAP from the intentional DRIVEL.

Yet, three people actually attempted it. They did their best—which, I think is PRETTY GOOD. Because proofreading this particular book would be tantamount to trying to win the US Tennis Open—playing with a spatula... while drunk... and naked.

So, a big thanks to Denise Robinson, Steve Fadie, and my wife, Nancy Matthews for giving it your best. And when all is said and doomed, YOUR best was no doubt better than MY best. Because...

MY best was THIS BOOK.

www.ingramcontent.com/pod-product-compliance
Lightning Source LLC
LaVergne TN
LVHW051545070426
835507LV00021B/2413

* 9 7 8 1 7 3 2 8 4 7 0 0 2 *